# Speechmaking

## The essential guide to effective public speaking

Susan Jones

POLITICO'S

First published in Great Britain 2004 by
Politico's Publishing, an imprint of
Methuen Publishing Limited
215 Vauxhall Bridge Road
London SW1V 1EJ

Copyright © Susan Jones 2004

Susan Jones has asserted her rights under the Copyright, Designs & Patents Act, 1988, to
be identified as the author of this work.

A CIP catalogue record for this book is available from the British Library.

ISBN 1 84275 109 3

Printed and bound in Great Britain by St. Edmundsbury Press, Bury St. Edmunds, Suffolk.

# Contents

# Acknowledgements

I have wanted to write this book for years, so for the encouragement to start it and to finish it I want to thank my husband, Ian Pettman.

For the opportunity to explore speeches, and for their patience during my trials and errors, I am grateful to the Rt Hon. Peter Lilley MP, to all my clients in government, the civil service, politics, business, education, science, charities, in the UK and internationally, and to all my students.

Special thanks are due to Christopher Jary and Sean Lusk at the Cabinet Office Centre for Management and Policy Studies. They are skilled speechwriters, inspiring teachers, great colleagues and contributors of many ideas in this book. Other ideas have come from Joan Baylis and Dr Kevin Crean.

To colleagues and friends who have provided inspiration and encouragement along the way I thank Philip Carr-Gomm, Dr Roger Sweeting, Adam and Rachel Bower, Chris Ogilvie, Rita Denby, Professor Ronald Hutton, Mary Spain; at Politico's, Sean Magee, Emma Musgrave and Hazel Orme; and my agent, John Pawsey.

Acknowledgement is due to those whose speeches appear in whole or in part in this book. The author and publisher have made every effort to seek copyright clearance, to be accurate, to give due credit and will gladly put right any errors or omissions in future editions.

I hope that this book will continue to be useful for many years to come. Many of the tools of speechmaking are ages old and are unlikely to go out of date. But there are always new tricks, and all busy speakers and speechwriters would like new ideas that will help. I would therefore be grateful for comments on this book, for examples of speeches, for ideas tried and tested for future editions. Please write to the publisher or:

sjones@dowrysquare.demon.co.uk

# One

# Speeches still matter . . .

Once the main tools of mass persuasion, speeches now compete with TV, radio, advertising and web-based media. Every new invention of information technology makes words travel further and faster, and reach more people more widely and more quickly. Text messages travel direct into hands that have not made any effort to reach for the words. The internet makes words available to millions at little cost almost as soon as they are written. But whenever there is something important to say, people still express it in speeches. They do so because they know that there is no better medium for showing a vision of a better world.

A good speech is an act of magic, when we, as listeners, surrender willingly to the spell cast by the speaker. Freed from the impediments of reality, we are open to the possibility of a greater good, higher ideals. We are not so much spurred on by the speaker as stirred up to recognise within ourselves what may be. As the words of a speech reach us, that which lay inert and unnamed is given life and energy. We make connections. Fact joins with feeling. We sense that something is resolved. We think well of the speaker for allowing us to grasp a new power in ourselves. The speaker, too, sees this. The audience relaxes, mutual trust is established. Listening to a good speech is satisfying. And perhaps we have all experienced it, on occasions great and small, at times of international crisis or at family celebrations.

We remember what was said and how it was put: a flash of sympathy for the Queen when she told us that 1992 had been 'an annus horribilis'; the 'new dawn' Tony Blair spoke of, the morning after he had won the 1997 general election; the defiant applause that spread outside Westminster Abbey after Earl Spencer's eulogy for his sister Diana at her funeral; and when President Clinton said in 1998 that he 'did not have sexual relations with that woman'. Wars, poverty, the atrocities of 11 September, confessions, resignations, retirements, elections have all been painted vividly in speeches. In the UK, devolution gave a once-in-a-lifetime opportunity to rid democratic institutions of speeches, perhaps using newer media, but the Scottish Parliament, the Welsh Assembly[1] and the Northern Ireland Assembly all chose to do most of their work through speeches.

However, many speeches are interminably tedious, and speakers say the wrong things. Week in, week out, audiences at conferences, events, launches and in Parliament doze through a day of boredom. Worse can happen. A speech by Tony Blair to the Women's Institute in 2000 earned him a slow hand clap. Speakers are wary of the sense of intimacy a speech demands. They fear a poor reception. They are often daunted by the idea that speechmaking, until recently, was considered a test of character: the gift of 'public speaking' was bestowed on one through birth, manners and education. It's no wonder that delivering a speech can be an ordeal.

Perhaps we have forgotten how to do it. Perhaps we have become so enthralled by high-tech gadgets – and spent so long learning how to use them – that we've neglected the low-tech skills such as speechmaking. A speech is the ultimate in low-tech use of words. It is scaled-up conversation, as simple as that.

The individualism of western society makes us demanding listeners. We want a speaker to understand our intelligence and to invite us to think, but not to dictate to us. We prefer to make up our own minds and to form our own opinions, so we want the tone of a speech to be consultative and to feel that we are involved in a conversation between ourselves and the speaker. We want to be transported out of normal reality. We want to like the speaker, and to know the common ground we share. And our passion for high-tech is cooling as we realise that a Powerpoint presentation is a poor substitute for a person talking to us with passion, sincerity and interest.

As speakers, we want speeches to change our world, whether in international politics, business or at local level. And the first requirement of a speaker is to gain the trust of their audience. Our trust in politicians and business leaders has been declining for decades. Society is disenchanted with and distrustful of authority. People aren't apathetic or apoliticised, but those in authority are seen as different. It's us-and-them, as though they are not of the same species. So above all, that's the challenge, to be seen as human. What's missing seems to be any connection with their audience's everyday lives, a common language, understanding and empathy, how small details fit into the big picture. All of those are wonderful ingredients for speeches. Or, looking at it another way, to meet the challenge of being seen to be human, a speech is a good medium to use. All speakers (and speechwriters) know that a good speech will boost their reputation in a way that almost nothing else can.

Speakers want their speeches to communicate with a wider audience, to go on speaking after they have sat down. Ideally, their words will be reported in newspapers, on TV and radio. Paradoxically the media have brought a new interest to speeches. Before the advent of the internet, the vast majority were lost as soon as they had been given. Unless a speech was delivered in Parliament or broadcast, the speaker kept their script or a transcript was made, the words were gone. What was said might never have been referred to again, except by a handful of specialists – mostly academics writing years after the event. Now many speeches appear on websites and are available to all who choose to read them.

I am a speechwriter. I am also a scientist by background. So the approach to speeches I will show you in this book is part art, part science. It does not depend on the innate skill of the speaker, or on literary genius; neither is it merely a dusting down of old skills of rhetoric. It relies heavily on what we know about how people communicate through the spoken word. It is based on the simple premises of cause and effect. It is low-tech. It produces the speeches that speakers want to make and audiences want to hear. As for magic in a speech, most of us can only aspire to it, and the more we chase it the more elusive it becomes. But we can all come close to it. A great speech is impossible to fake: no matter how good the writer, it will only work if the speaker is honest, sincere and every word is their own. Only the person delivering the speech can be the expert in meaning what they say and saying what they mean.

Great speakers of the past relied on literary genius, and those who have it can still create magic in a speech. But it is not the only way. If we discard the idea of a speech as a literary art form and define it as applied psychology, we can construct speeches that are far more predictable in their effects. Audiences will sit entranced for hours by a good comedian, and comedians don't, on the whole, rely on literary genius: they rely on their subject matter and an understanding of how audiences react to the spoken word, and use them to generate the reaction they want. They know the speech patterns that produce laughter. We can apply some of the same processes – based on audience observation and reaction – as an approach to speechmaking.

A speech is different from a presentation. Both convey a message, but only a speech '. . . connects the speaker, the audience, the time and the place'[2] as Tony Benn has reminded us. In a speech the focus is the speaker; in a presentation it is the subject. In a presentation the identity of the speaker may be irrelevant: they may give no more than a commentary on a series of slides, a presentation doesn't even have to be given live. A speechmaker is generally of superior status to their audience while someone making a presentation is often talking to superiors: the chairman reporting the firm's annual results to share-holders is making a speech, but the financial controller giving the same results to the board is making a presentation. The chairman and the financial controller use the same information but offer different perspectives. Schoolteachers or college lecturers are also superior to their audience, but in teaching they do not make speeches: the message they convey belongs to a syllabus. The message of a speech is the speaker's own. Most people say that the difference between a speech and a presentation is that a presentation is supported by visual aids, from a few slides to a theatrical spectacular. In a speech, all eyes are on the speaker.

Above all though, the main difference between speeches and presentations is of purpose and effect. Speeches are excellent to persuade, inspire and entertain, but are of little use in imparting information. Presentations – good ones at least – are more about information, less about persuasion and seldom entertain or inspire.

The reality on most occasions is often more of a hybrid. Lord Hutton's statement[3] on the publication of his report of the inquiry into the death of weapons expert Dr David Kelly, following the war in Iraq, was part speech, part presentation. As a speech, it spoke to the wider public audience, all eyes were on the speaker, who included his own opinion. As a presentation, it spoke to the Government, who had commissioned the report, it didn't attempt to entertain, the speaker scarcely glanced at his audience and most of what he had to say was information rather than opinion.

For the purposes of this book, a speech is delivered by one person to an audience, with their own message and without props.

## SPEECH OR PRESENTATION?

| Speech | Presentation |
|---|---|
| Focus is on the speaker | Focus is on the subject |
| Message is speaker's own | Message may not be speaker's own |
| Better for inspiring, persuading | Better for informing |
| Speaker superior to audience | Speaker inferior to audience |

Expert speakers understand the power they wield with a speech, so use this medium in their communication strategy to further their business or political aims. They speak frequently, but prefer major occasions and are careful not to accept too many minor engagements. The rest of us speak only when we have to or in response to an invitation.

Successful speakers gain confidence from their authority over the subject matter. They prepare from all angles and know far more about the subject than they will need to mention. The time spent in preparation is devoted mostly to getting to grips with their subject and the research. The rest of us tend to assume that our elaborate Powerpoint presentation (or a pile of slides) will provide us with the necessary confidence.

The inexperienced speaker tends to concentrate on what they want to say, while the experienced speaker balances this with what the audience wants to hear. Expert speakers know what to say and how to say it. But if you ask a naturally talented speaker how they craft their speeches many will be unable to tell you. It is not because they are unwilling to divulge the secret, but because they genuinely don't know.

In fact, much of what naturally effective speakers do is contrary to perceived wisdom. On a presentation-skills course, you may be advised to 'Tell them what you are going to tell them, tell them, then tell them what you've told them.' But no audience would want to listen to a speech like that: it would be too dull and predictable. 'Avoid long sentences' – no great orator does. 'Learn from an actor': if that were true, all Oscar acceptance speeches would be brilliant, but they rarely are. Actors seem to have just as much trouble as the rest of us at playing themselves. US President Ronald Reagan, who was an actor, employed a speechwriter. 'Read great speeches': they may be inspiring, but they may make the goal of giving a good-enough speech seem as unattainable as reaching the summit of Everest. Anyway, speeches sometimes become great only with the benefit of hindsight – Abraham Lincoln's Gettysburg address fell flat on the day.

Speakers refine their craft with practice and rehearsal. They don't do drama training, but they work hard at developing a personal style. They don't follow a formula. They don't find it easy and they all get nervous – but they prepare thoroughly.

Many books on speeches say that anyone can become a great speaker, and that the starting point is improving yourself. A book on public speaking published fifty years ago trumpeted: 'Everything hangs on the personality. If he is muddle–witted, no power can make him argue clearly on the platform or anywhere else. Public speaking is the art of self-expression by means of word and if the self to be expressed is bumptious, unimaginative and insincere, every one of these vices and defects will be apparent in the speaking.'[4] That would only put most of us off trying, it promotes the wrong approach. A successful speaker starts with the audience, and what audiences like to hear in speeches, rather than him- or herself; the rest is relatively easy. In this book I will show you how speakers achieve success and I hope you will be inspired to have a go.

One short-cut is to use a speechwriter. The good speechwriter is anonymous and I doubt that a great speech has ever been written entirely by someone other than the speaker. The best a speechwriter can do is to act as an extension to the client, seeing and hearing for them and, at best, knowing what they are thinking before they think it. A speechwriter will tune in to the same wavelength as the speaker and draft in a way that they will recognise as their own. There are few professional speechwriters, but thousands of civil servants, junior MPs, special advisers, business managers, assistants and secretaries write speeches for their bosses. They have neither training nor practice in this specialist task, and yet when they have to do it, the result is often high profile. This book is for them, too.

For over ten years my life has been dominated by speeches, and I shall illustrate this book with extracts from many speeches – most of them recent, most of them well-known. All show how and why the speaker achieved their effect.

Speeches have important jobs to do – for the world, the country, business, an organisation, the community, family and friends. They can summon peace, win votes in Parliament, raise funds for worthy causes and unite families. We will mention only in passing the after-dinner speaking circuit, with its professional entertainers, and motivational gurus who tend to give the same speech on each occasion. I don't include speaking at the Bar, because law isn't my expertise.

From time to time, many of us have a chance of shaping the world through a speech. I hope this book will help you to do that. And for those who listen to and read speeches, I hope that by revealing some of the secrets of how they work, this book will add to your enjoyment but take away none of the magic.

# Two

# What makes a good speech and how to build one

We are such good judges of speeches that when we listen to one, within a split second we can identify whether it is good and indicate this to the speaker with applause, laughter or simply our attention. So, we must know what makes a good speech. Yet people often say they wouldn't know where to start building a speech.

## What is a good speech?

The success, or otherwise, of a speech is instantaneous. From the moment the first words are uttered, the audience is assessing it. The speaker picks up their reaction and then – all being well – any listening journalists get to work with TV, radio and newspaper coverage. In other areas of work, like policy implementation, project management or product development, it may be weeks, months or years before their effectiveness can be judged. I asked fifty people who attended my speechwriting courses what makes a successful speech: the table that follows records their comments.

## Indicators of a good speech

### For the audience

'Audience is attentive'

'Audience applauds'

'Audience stays awake, there's no snoring'

'Nods in agreement'

'Audience takes notes'

'There's a reaction to every sentence'

'Everyone laughs'

'Nobody heckles'

'No sighs'

'No coughing'

'No missiles!'

'Audience looks interested'

'Grabs and keeps attention all the way through'

'It's like a conversation with the audience'

'Worth talking about it afterwards'

'Can repeat phrases from it afterwards'

'Audience does something after the speech in response – votes, decides'

'Audience asks questions'

### For the speaker

'The script is easy to read'

'Deliverable'

'Speaker doesn't stumble over script'

'Suits the speaker'

'Contains terminology the speaker uses'

'No exclusive language the audience wouldn't use'

'Right length'

'Says something new'

'The technology works'

'The objectives are achieved for the speaker'

'The objectives are achieved for the speaker's organisation'

'The audience is the right one for the speech'

'Speaker looks as though they are enjoying doing the speech'

'Shows speaker in best light'

**Wider success**

'Speaker is invited to media interviews'
'Reported short-term, reported long-term'
'Press coverage is positive'
'Press coverage is accurate, approving'
'Makes a headline'
'Spin-off articles'
'It becomes permanent'
'Seen by a wide audience'
'Gains peer approval'
'Wins vote'
'The organisers of the event are happy'

**The speechwriter's perspective**

'The applause came where I expected it'
'Speaker is happy'
'Thanks from speaker'
'Few changes from draft'
'Lots of good changes by speaker'
'Made the point it was supposed to make'
'Met its objective'
'Don't have to go back and explain it'
'Shouldn't have to spend the next week rescuing the situation'

The survey shows that even relatively inexperienced speechwriters have no trouble in recognising a good speech. All they have to learn is how to elicit applause, how to make their speech interesting and how to make headlines. Then they will know how to make speeches work.

The table tells us that both speaker and audience have some fairly basic requirements of a speech. For the speaker it should at least be 'sayable'. Yet one of the main complaints I hear from speakers for whom others write speeches is that the draft put in front of them cannot be read aloud. The audience wants, above all else, to 'stay awake'. Humour is an optional extra. Audiences prize honesty and sincerity. They also like to know that the speaker is enjoying him- or herself. Many speakers, however, say that the best way to improve their speeches would be with humour. Some points appear to conflict. For example, 'Few changes from draft' and 'Lots of good changes by speaker'. If the speaker didn't change a word of a speech-writer's draft, it might have been perfect. Or it may be that they delivered it without enough preparation. If the final speech bore no resemblance to the draft, perhaps the draft was unsatisfactory. It is more likely that the speaker found it helpful in stimulating their own thoughts – certainly it saved them time on research and putting down the first words on paper. Some speakers rewrite every word – it's their way of learning their lines. One speaker said to me, 'Good – the draft is now at the stage where I can completely rewrite it.' It was a compliment, although others within earshot weren't too sure of that!

### What's interesting?

Tolstoy said, 'All happy families resemble one another. Each unhappy family is unhappy in its own way.'[1] Speeches are the opposite: every

successful speech, whatever its mood, is successful in its own way. It's
a one-off, with a unique sparkle. On the other hand, all unsuccessful
speeches resemble each other: they are too long, too abstract, too
disorganised, too impersonal, too unsympathetic to the audience, too
inhibited. They are dull – and too numerous.

An effective speechmaker has an instinctive feel for what's interesting. To start with, it's helpful to see the world as divided into three
levels. Global concerns and universal values are at the top. This is the
big picture, and there is something for everyone in it. The world of
the individual, the unique and personal, is at the bottom. The top
and bottom levels are interesting, especially when you relate the two
by showing how the actions of one individual matter to the world.
The middle level is dull; this is the world of civil servants and
managers, of big numbers, policy, projects, initiatives, campaigns,
bureaucracy, where people are lumped together and the questions
how, where and when are answered. It is important, but it only
becomes interesting when explored from above and below.

## A WORLD OF INTEREST

| | |
|---|---|
| Universal, global, all humanity, big picture, theory, big questions. Why? | Interesting |
| Policy, groups of people, generalisations, statistics, budgets, management. How? Where? When? | Dull |
| The individual. The real thing. Real numbers. The unique. The particular. Who? What? | Interesting |

The message for speechwriters is clear: if you want to be interesting, focus on the top and bottom levels, relate the universal to the particular, and keep well away from the dull grey area in the middle. UN Secretary General Kofi Annan achieved this in his Nobel lecture of December 2001:

> *Scientists tell us that the world of nature is so small and interdependent that a butterfly flapping its wings in the Amazon rainforest can generate a violent storm on the other side of the earth. This principle is known as the 'Butterfly Effect'. Today we realise, perhaps more than ever, that the world of human activity also has its own 'Butterfly Effect' – for better or for worse. We have entered the third millennium through a gate of fire. If today, after the horror of 11 September, we see better, and we see further – we will realise that humanity is indivisible. New threats make no distinction between races, nations or regions. A new insecurity has entered every mind, regardless of wealth or status. A deeper awareness of the bonds that bind us all – in pain as in prosperity – has gripped young and old.*[2]

Of course it is an advantage if the world is the territory of a speech. But I doubt if the people of Warrington found much of interest in what John Prescott said on 4 November 2003:

> *I am delighted to be in Warrington today to launch our campaign . . . Its aim is to explain what an elected regional assembly would mean for you, the people of this region. Since 1997 we have made significant steps towards the devolution of power away from Whitehall and Westminster to the people of this country . . . Now it is the turn of the English regions. We*

*said we would strengthen the English regions. And we have. We
have boosted economic growth by setting up the regional development agencies. We have strengthened the government offices.
And we have established regional chambers in all our regions . . .
That is why we are in Warrington today. We're launching an
information campaign . . .*[3]

## What is the speech for?

The first step in making a speech is to give it a purpose. The purpose
of John Prescott's speech, above, seems to have been to launch an
information campaign – which doesn't sound interesting. Perhaps a
more engaging purpose would have been to explain why a regional
assembly is a Good Thing and the benefits that their own would
bring to people who live in the North West.

The speaker must know the purpose of the speech so that they can
hone a central idea and speak up for it. A speech is never about
something, always for something. It helps to sum up the purpose in
a sentence: 'The purpose of my speech is to . . .'

- '. . . win the vote'
- '. . . be elected'
- '. . . persuade the audience that . . .'
- '. . . inspire the audience to . . .'
- '. . . make the audience feel good about . . .'
- '. . . launch a ship.'

To know what a speech is for makes the rest of the preparation much
easier. If you start to write it knowing only what it is 'about', the task
is endless – there will always be something more to say on any
subject.

Where any speech is concerned, the audience may have more interest in the speaker than in what he or she is saying. They have come to see the speaker as much as hear them. It may be enough for the purpose of the speech to be seen to be human.

## Design and build

Few of us remember the shape and structure of a speech we have heard. We may remember snippets of content or our impressions of the speaker, our reactions to the argument or the mood of the audience, and these are the important elements to take away. Why should a speaker give their speech a framework? Because without one, their words will be difficult to absorb. The audience will get no further than the last point that made sense to them. The bigger the speech, the stronger the structure should be to hold it all together.

An audience listens only if it is in its interest to listen, and there are many claims on our attention. When we listen to the spoken word, we take in two or three words per second. But the brain works faster than that, because it is processing input from the other senses, sight, smell, touch, taste, and constantly throwing up new thoughts and feelings. At every moment, it is looking for something to do and won't rest until it finds it. After every few words during a speech, something else competes for the listener's attention. Will that attention go to the speech or elsewhere? A listener doesn't decide, at the beginning of a speech , 'Right, I'm going to listen to every word', they think, 'OK, I'll give you a chance, and if what I hear gains my attention I will give you a bit more.' As soon as the speaker says something unclear or hard to understand, the audience may switch off. If the speaker manages to gain only half of a listener's attention, a curious thing happens: the listener falls asleep. This, as any reader of bedtime stories knows, is a skill in itself, related to hypnosis.

## The attention slide

There is no better way to send a roomful of people to sleep – cheaply, easily, legally and quickly – than to inflict on them an averagely dull speech. The lower curve on this graph shows the pattern of audience attention during a typical twenty-minute speech.

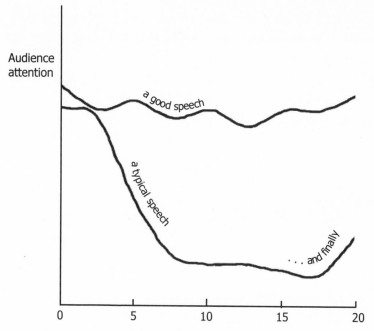

The pattern of audience attention during a 20 minute speech

Audience attention:
- is highest at the beginning of a speech
- slides after only a few minutes
- rises towards the end, but only if the speaker signals that the end is in sight by saying '. . . and finally . . .'

The pattern is fairly standard for all speeches. The audience wants to pay attention, but the trial period is short – as you will see when you watch any audience and notice how its attention sags visibly. A boring speech will have lost its audience within thirty seconds of the start.

Attention naturally follows interest. If what the audience hears is of no interest, their attention instantly goes to something that is – lunch, a business problem, daydreaming – or, as once happened to me in 10 Downing Street, the thick layer of dust on the furniture. Unless something happens to bring their attention back to the speech, they will soon be asleep. This is not what anyone wants. So the pattern of audience attention has some important implications for the structure and content of a speech:

- The beginning must grab the audience's attention.
- The middle must work hard to maintain their attention.
- The end of the speech must have a build up so that attention at the end is high.

## Where to put the 'news'

The 'news' should be introduced at the beginning, where attention is highest. There is, of course, an argument for putting it at the end, but this only works where it has been trailed in advance of the speech. When the chancellor, Gordon Brown, announced the extra £4 billion spending on the NHS in the 2000 Budget, the announcement came in the final two minutes of his fifty-six-minute speech. Members of the House waited with full attention during the whole speech because they were expecting it. It is a clever tactic to keep the audience's attention, but few of us have such important news to announce. And even when we have, there's the question of how to use the rest of the speech. The news is the main subject of the speech so surely there is plenty to talk about.

## Where to put the less-than-interesting sections

All experienced speakers know that sometimes, for reasons of diplomacy, strategy or even law, they must include dull material. The pattern tells us that any boring bits should be in the middle when audience attention is low. Should you ever need to 'lose' content in a speech, put it in the middle and express it in a low-key way (see page 67–68). No one will notice it was there, unless they look for it. If the speaker wants attention to remain high throughout a speech, something interesting must happen every few seconds, which is why detailed drafting is so important.

In practice, few speakers start their preparation with a definite structure in mind. It tends to emerge during the research process and early drafting. The bigger the speech, the longer this takes. John Major gives an insight into the process most speakers go through: 'When writing a speech you can start anywhere – even with the conclusion. I used to turn over the points I wanted to make until they formed a pattern, and then the rest would fall into place.' And, like most of us, he found that: 'The hardest parts of a speech are the first and last paragraphs.'[4]

## The first few words

This is the first place to make a connection with the audience: the speaker wants the audience to be on the same side, to feel a common purpose or belonging, to give them nothing, at least for a moment, with which to disagree.

## The 'bridge'

It sometimes helps to start a speech with two introductions:

The words of the first are like steps on a bridge that leads towards the audience. 'I'm delighted to be here . . .' is a cliché, but it links the time, the place and the occasion. Earl Spencer achieved this in the opening words of his eulogy for his sister, Diana, Princess of Wales: 'I stand before you today the representative of a family in grief, in a country in mourning before a world in shock.' [5]

On most occasions, though, it is enough to say something nice, something flattering. Thank the audience, praise, admire or welcome them, as individuals or a group. Even 'I'm delighted to be here' becomes more interesting if you add 'I'm delighted to be here, on my first visit to Blackpool'. In his speech to the 2002 Labour Party Conference, Bill Clinton said:

> *I am trying to imagine what in the world I am doing here. I have never been to Blackpool before. I had never been to the McDonald's in Blackpool before. I like the city, I like the weather, and I understand I may have brought it; if so I will take credit for any good thing I can, these days. I want you to know that I am honoured to be here. I did very much enjoy the opportunity of touring around the city last night; I did like McDonald's, I did like the people who came up and said hello. I welcome the invitation and I thank you for the warm applause when I came in. I accepted when Prime Minister Blair invited me to come because he and Cherie are old friends, because I love this country and feel deeply indebted to it. It gave me two of the best years of my life and I think my daughter is getting two of the best years of her life here as well.* [6]

Twelve compliments in one paragraph!

The first priority is to be nice, and only the second to be clever. Give special attention to the way you step on to the bridge when your status with the audience is unclear, when the audience isn't united, when you are a guest or a host, accepting or presenting an award.

The second introduction can bring in the subject matter with the main thesis of the speech: 'I have chosen to address the House first on why I cannot support a war without international agreement or domestic support.'[7]

You can combine the two parts of the bridge, as Mark Antony does when he declares in Shakespeare's *Julius Caesar*, 'Friends, Romans, countrymen; lend me your ears, I come to bury Caesar not to praise him.' 'Friends, Romans, countrymen,' takes a step towards the audience, 'I come to bury Caesar not to praise him' reaches the other side, and the territory of what he will go on to say.

Sometimes it is possible to span the bridge in one step – to combine the greeting with the main subject. It's more difficult, but the opportunity occasionally presents itself, as it did here, in the memorial address given by the Roman Catholic Archbishop of Liverpool for the cockler-pickers drowned in Morecambe Bay in 2004:

> *The tapestry brought to the Cathedral from St Mary's Church, Morecambe, was designed by Ray Schofield. There is no doubt what it portrays: Simon Peter and his companions on the Sea of Galilee, hauling in a net filled to breaking point with fish. But there is no less doubt that the colours of the sky and sea reflecting the sky are those of sunset over Morecambe Bay, and the hills are unmistakably those of the Lake District. So the tapestry sets the scene for us. We may begin with this word of*

> *Peter to Jesus: 'We worked hard all night, we laboured until breaking point.' I think of the emergency services . . .*[8]

## The straight-to-the-point start

If circumstances, time or place allow, or the subject matter is important enough, it may be best to forgo any preliminaries. For example, George Bush's radio address immediately after the events of 11 September 2001 began: 'This weekend I am engaged in extensive sessions with members of my National Security Council, as we plan a comprehensive assault on terrorism. This will be a different kind of conflict against a different kind of enemy.'[9]

## 'Agree, But, So . . .'

In the early stages of a putting together a speech we generally know what we want to talk about but not necessarily what we want to say. The next structure gets round that: it has widespread application in journalism, for articles, features, editorials, documentaries in TV, radio and newspapers, and is one of the most useful starting points for a speech. Try this one before you choose any other.[10]

First the speaker makes a statement of fact about the current situation, something the audience can agree with. Then he or she presents a complication on that situation, adding a 'but' to the first statement. This leads the listener to question 'So?' and the rest of the speech answers them. George Bush used this structure in announcing that the US would attack Afghanistan in 2001. First he set out the 'agree' statement: 'More than two weeks ago, I gave Taleban leaders a series of clear and specific demands: close terrorist training camps; hand over leaders of the al-Qaeda network; and return all foreign nationals, including American citizens unjustly detained in your country.' Then came the 'but': 'None of these demands were met.'

'So?'

Bush supplied the answer: 'And now the Taleban will pay a price.'[11]

The rest of the speech set out the plans for military action.

To arrive at the best 'Agree, But, So' structure with your own material, ask yourself the following questions:

1. 'Agree' statement: what is the most interesting statement of fact about the situation, and about which we can all agree – or, at least, not disagree?
2. 'But' qualification: what is the biggest and most interesting discrepancy in the situation? For example, 'but the situation doesn't hold true when . . .'; 'but the situation went wrong . . .'; 'but the situation didn't turn out as we expected . . .'; 'but the situation was different from how it looked'
3. 'So?' question: what is the best that can be said about where the subject of the speech is heading?

This formula is invaluable in dealing with controversy, or when the speech is to be delivered to a divided audience, because speaker and audience start in the same place. It is the classic start to story-telling. It can identify the most interesting start to a speech and can help you to find the best route through the most unprepossessing of material.

## Begin with a joke?

A questionable piece of advice. Time at the start of a speech is precious. Many speeches won't be about a laughing matter. Long anecdotes don't work because they don't achieve instant connection with the audience. A joke that falls flat is the worst possible start to a speech. It may be better advice to begin by showing you have a sense of humour, or to go straight to what you want to say.

Alternatives to jokes include an expression of personal feeling, honest self-revelation and, especially, self-deprecation. Self-effacing humour scores at the start of a speech. Nelson Mandela, visiting the 2000 Labour Party Conference in the midst of the row about the seventy-five pence increase in British state pensions, began by teasing the audience that they were only there because they wanted 'to see what a pensioner from the Commonwealth looks like'. It was apt, self-effacing and funny.

## The controversial statement

'If I say something controversial, I'll get the audience hooked': it may work with some, but antagonise others. Even experienced speakers come unstuck with controversial statements. At the 1999 Labour Party Conference, the backdrop, in Tony Blair's own hand-writing, read, 'Labour for the many not the few.' He started his speech by apologising for being late, 'but it's all those hunting horns outside the window. Still, here goes, tally ho' and 'what a great day for foxes'. He tried to unite his audience in the auditorium against the protestors outside, but alienated the audience beyond. Blair's comments at the start of a speech have often put part or all of an audience against him, which is at odds with his desire for inclusivity.

## The 'Letter from America' start

Alistair Cooke often started his Letters from America with a hook such as this one from a broadcast a year before he died: 'Edging myself into bed the other night and licking my lips . . .'[12]

Immediately he had our attention and kept it until he returned to the original subject and we saw how it all linked together. In this case he was looking forward to reading a new book, a biography of a civil servant that related to the prospect of war in Iraq. The technique is called 'bracketing', but beware of using it if your speech is likely to be subject to an editorial committee: you may find that a last-minute change removes one of the references, leaving the other stranded. It takes skill, confidence and control over the draft to bring it off. Some comedians, such as Billy Connolly, run two stories in parallel, switching back and forth between the two and never forgetting where they left off. Wonderful to listen to, but not for novices.

The main choice to make at the beginning of a speech is between the comfort of the familiar and the memorability of the unusual. Your own judgement will tell you which is best. You may also want to include welcoming courtesies, self-identification, an indication of where you are heading and your rules of the road (for example, if you will allow questions at the end). Try to keep opening remarks to the minimum or ask someone else to warm up the audience. It is tempting to spend time at the beginning of a speech doing a round of thank yous (Oscar speeches seldom get beyond that) but it may be better to bring them in near the end. At the point when attention may be flagging, thank some of the audience by name – it'll have the sleepiest among them paying attention again.

## How not to start a speech

In my experience, novice speechwriters seem to opt for the riskiest opening words. They love rambling jokes, controversial statements, bracketing and anything off-the-wall. Worst of all is to ask forgiveness, permission or sympathy. None will be forthcoming. The audience does not want to hear how difficult it is to give a speech, why you haven't prepared anything or how bad you are at it. Recently, I heard a chief executive start with: 'This wasn't my idea. I was inveigled into this speech.'

One 'how-to' book on speeches[13] includes over twenty sample speeches that begin with:

- 'I don't want to make a speech'
- '. . . sitting on this platform feeling sorry for myself because I had to make a speech'
- 'Before I present the prizes, I am expected to make a speech. You probably think that is hard on you but I assure you it is much harder on me'
- 'We are here tonight to be entertained. My remarks do not come under this heading.'

Perhaps the idea is to convey humility, but it sounds weak and may turn a speaker into their audience's victim.

If the speech's first words fail to make contact with the audience, it will falter. Even professionals sometimes get off to a bad start. In December 2002 Cherie Blair's statement apologising for the embarassment caused by her involvement with a convicted fraudster was poorly received. How much better it would have been if her first few words had shown more understanding of the audience and less of her own position:

> *In view of all the controversy around me at the moment I hope you don't mind me using this event to say a few words. You can't have failed to notice that there's been a lot of allegations about me and I haven't said anything, but when I got back to Downing Street today and discovered that some of the press are*

*effectively suggesting that I tried to influence a judge I knew
that the time had come for me to say something. It is not fair to
Tony or to the Government that the entire focus of political
debate at the moment is about me. I know I'm in a very special
position, I'm the wife of the Prime Minister, I have an interesting job and a wonderful family, but I also know I am not
Superwoman. The reality of my daily life is that I'm juggling a
lot of balls in the air. Some of you must experience that.*[14]

Lack of preparation time didn't help. It was reported that:

*Appropriately for a woman who says she has to juggle too many
balls, the Prime Minister's wife had to host a children's party
before she could concentrate on her speech. She spent most of
Tuesday afternoon handing out chocolate cake to seventy
children and it was not until five thirty p.m. – an hour before
she was due to speak – that she sat down, at her own computer
in the Blairs' Downing Street flat, to write the statement.*[15]

## 'Off the peg' structures

### The simple speech – three points

Tony Blair's speech on the morning after the death of Diana, Princess of Wales, gave some sort of order to the confusion of emotion that had built up over just a few hours. We remember his spontaneity, body language, dress, and his trademark mix of informality and tradition, especially in his closing words, 'the People's Princess'. By any standards, this was a big speech, setting a tone which was unmatched in the days that followed by the Queen, the leader of the opposition, William Hague, and former Prime Minister John Major. Blair delivered his speech apparently impromptu, able to do so because it was short, less than 300 words, and simply structured, with just three points related to time – the present, the past, the future:

> *I feel like everyone else in the country today – utterly devastated. Our thoughts and prayers are with Princess Diana's family – in particular her two sons, two boys – our hearts go out to them. We are today a nation, in Britain, in a state of shock, in mourning, in grief that is so deeply painful for us.*
>
> *She was a wonderful and warm human being. Though her own life was often touched sadly by tragedy, she touched the lives of so many others in Britain and throughout the world with joy and with comfort. How many times shall we remember her, in how many different ways, with the sick, the dying, with children, with the needy? With just a look or a gesture that spoke so much more than words, she would reveal to all of us the depth of her compassion and her humanity. We know how difficult things were for her from time to time. I am*

*sure we can only guess at that. But people everywhere, not just here in Britain but everywhere, kept faith with Princess Diana. They liked her, they loved her, they regarded her as one of the people.*

*She was the People's Princess and that is how she will stay, how she will remain in our hearts and memories for ever.*[16]

This structure, of present, past, future, is perhaps the most useful in all speechmaking. In business and politics, it neatly frames administrative and political change: Where are we now? How did we get to that situation? Where are we going? At weddings, on birthdays and at funerals it tells the story of the relationships we celebrate. Most short speeches need be no more complicated. Notice that the end of the speech is about the future, which is where nearly all speeches lead. The order of the early parts may change: to past, present, future. In 1963, for one of the most famous speeches ever, Martin Luther King used this format: 'Five score years ago, a great American . . . signed the Emancipation Proclamation [past]. But one hundred years later, we must face the tragic fact that the Negro is still not free . . . [present] . . . I have a dream . . . [future]'[17]

For most of us, and especially when we make an impromptu speech, three points – about present, past and future – will provide a framework for a pleasant speech that requires the minimum in preparation. It may be helpful to think ahead to the next event at which you may be called upon to 'say a few words'. Prepare a simple structure, based on three points that you can remember without notes.

In traditional speech terminology, these three parts equate to the preoration, perioration, peroration or you can think of a speech as a steam train: an engine at the front to generate a good head of steam, the carriages in the middle containing your message, and a guard's van at the rear as a strong conclusion.

Any spoken address or report needs a firm framework. The BBC is constantly trying to improve the weather forecast while keeping it short. It moves backwards and forwards in time, comparing yesterday with today and tomorrow; to avoid regional bias, the geographical route changes from day to day. That is why it is so easy – and infuriating – to miss what you were listening for. Here is an example:

> *For Eastern England, the Midlands and the West Country it will be dull and cloudy, a repeat of yesterday, with some patchy mist and hill fog and pockets of rain and drizzle. Temperatures are six degrees in Newcastle, seven degrees Celsius in London, with no change through the rest of the day. Tonight remains cloudy for most with some showers and more broken cloud pushing in from the east. In the south, together with the southeast of England and Wales, there is a risk of frost and fog. Heading west now, temperatures in Liverpool are only five degrees, eight degrees in Cardiff. Most places are bright enough with a little hazy sunshine. We are going to have some patches of fog noticeably around Irish Sea coasts and the west coast of Wales. Tonight we'll see fog becoming more widespread with some drizzle here or there by morning and temperatures of two degrees. Moving northwards into Northern Ireland where it is sunny and pleasant for many parts with temperatures nearer seven or eight, fog will thicken overnight with frost for most of Northern Ireland with temperatures of minus one or minus two. Now for Scotland, many parts will see some sunshine through the rest of the day, with temperatures of seven in Glasgow, six in Aberdeen. Eastern areas of Scotland will see more cloud. It is going to thicken particularly overnight giving some pockets of drizzle. Western areas overnight will have some*

*patchy fog, limited by a southerly breeze with temperatures of minus 1.*[18]

Will it be foggy in Sussex? Where will there be a frost? Who will get the best of the sunshine? The answers will be hard to find unless you reread the passage.

### One thesis, three points, a conclusion

The three points can be elevated by adding a thesis and a conclusion. Decide what you most want to say and make that your thesis. Then say three things about it. State your conclusion.

In a speech on systems of health-care funding to the Social Market Foundation before the 2002 Budget, Gordon Brown adopted a three-point structure: 'to examine the main alternatives [to general taxation] – user charges, private insurance and social insurance' against three tests of equity, efficiency and cost, and concluding in favour of social insurance via the NHS. It was an elegant development of a simple structure into a significant think-piece speech.

### The hero's journey

We are told that a story should have a beginning, a middle and an end, but there's a good reason for avoiding this formula because it starts in the past, which is invariably less interesting than the present. So, how do we tell a story? We need characters and a plot. All the best stories have a hero or heroine – a person or, perhaps, a country, a community, a policy, a product, a value or an action. The hero has an adventure, often involving a journey, quest or challenge, with a satisfactory resolution.

The skill is in choosing the best story, which, as any child will tell you, is the one they already know. But when a speaker wants to say something new, the choice of story is a fine balance between the two. If it's too well known, the audience switches off; too obscure, they find it hard to grasp the point.

Many stories start with the 'agree, but, so' formula. The introduction states a situation the reader accepts and agrees to. This is the function of the classic story opening 'once upon a time . . .'. The 'but', the complication, follows, then 'so' leads to a question raised by the complication. The rest of the story answers the question. It works just as well for

*Once upon a time there was a girl named Cinderella.* – Agree

*Her two ugly sisters wouldn't let her go to the ball.* – But

*How was Cinderella going to get to the ball?* – So?

as it does for

*The White Paper gives new powers to local communities.* – Agree

*If those powers are to work, we will need a new consultative framework.* – But

*What will that framework look like?* – So?

Once into the story, let the characters interact with the setting. Appeal to the senses. Give the emotional commentary. Involve the audience by responding to their reactions. A story is an efficient way to help an audience grasp the significance of what is being said, because the storyteller holds up for examination various knowns and unknowns to guide them to the conclusion.

In his 2001 Oscar acceptance speech for Best Actor in the film *Gladiator*, Russell Crowe overcame the difficulty of making himself the hero of his story by modestly making himself the outsider to the audience, siding with the underdog: 'When you grow up in the suburbs of Sydney or Auckland or Newcastle, like Ridley [Scott] or Jamie Bell, or the suburbs of anywhere, a dream like this seems kind of ludicrous and unobtainable. But this moment is directly connected to those childhood imaginings. And for anybody who's on the downside of advantage, and relying purely on courage, it's possible.'

## The Gift

It helps some speakers to feel that they are offering a gift to the audience. Perhaps this was in Margaret Thatcher's mind when she delivered her 'Let me give you my vision'[19] speech. A personal commitment, a new idea, an encouragement or inspiration can all form the basis of a speech. The Gift, as a speech structure, is useful when viewing a new installation, opening a building, presenting ideas at a policy forum or in any situation where the speaker wants to leave their mark, but also at funerals and memorial services where the intention is to evoke a memory of the individual who has died.

## The 'Magic Formula' – and its converse 'Order out of Chaos'

One of the most persuasive structures we can use in a speech is also one of the most used techniques in advertising. Early in the 20th century, Dale Carnegie came up with the 'Magic Formula'.[20] It starts with an 'Example', an incident, occurrence or state of being, followed by the 'Point', in which you tell the audience what you want them to do, if necessary add the 'Reason' – why you want them to do it – and the 'Highlight', which is the advantage or benefit to be gained. Examples of this appear in almost any direct marketing letter: 'Do you want the freedom, peace of mind and savings offered by no other credit card?' it begins. Then comes the Point: 'Apply now for our Platinum Credit Card.' The rest of the letter highlights the benefits to be gained: 'Forget about high interest on purchases and balance transfers, enjoy an exceptional range of credit card services, and if that's not enough, how does a low annual rate of 13 per cent suit you?'

'Order out of Chaos' is the other side of the Magic Formula. This starts by pointing to an undesirable state of being, the chaotic, the faulty, the not quite right, and outlines the problems until the audience is convinced that something should be done. The rest of the speech is about how to put things right, and the speech is successful if the speaker convinces the audience that order will indeed be brought out of chaos. This formula works well when the speaker wishes to introduce changes in policy or procedure, including parliamentary legislation. It can make even the most unprepossessing material worth listening to. The speech to introduce the second reading of the Recovery of Benefits Bill 1997, the most obscure Act of Parliament I have worked on, started by stating the situation about which the speaker and listener might at that point agree, which was that the Bill dealt with a less well-known piece of legislation about compensation for injuries. It went on to list a catalogue of problems – some people were being compensated twice for the same injury, some victims weren't receiving compensation for pain and suffering, and many were settling for less than the true value of their suffering – then set out how to put them right, the reforms and the cost. The Bill comfortably won the vote.

## Pyramids

The human ear can process a maximum of five pieces of information at any one time and the listener remember what has been said. Thus, three to five points are suitable for most short speeches. But in bigger, longer speeches, there will be far more points and the speaker must work harder to help the listener organise the information. The mind does this either by taking individual pieces of information 'bottom-up' and building from them a structure of ideas, or by working 'top-down' within an overall idea, then finding the pieces of information from which the idea is put together. Either way, the common structure is the pyramid.

If there are six reasons for a course of action, which would be too many for the listener to take in, it is best to split the list into two groups of three, or one of two and one of four – say, one group of financial points, the other practical. Of course, in writing the speech you could start at the top, say what action you recommend, then give the reasons. Or you could start with the reasons, then conclude with the recommendation. Top-down is 'push', bottom-up is 'pull'.

The starting point is likely to be an assorted list of points for possible inclusion, which should be arranged according to the relationships between them. Most big speeches are about policy, action or both and you should aim high with the biggest top-down idea, then go through the judgements as to whether you will 'push' your reasoning or 'pull' it.

Some speakers find it helpful to write each point of the speech on a small card, then arrange them in a pyramid. It's a good way to reveal any gaps in the reasoning.

Every point of a speech should fit into a pyramid structure made of blocks with no more than five sections. The only exception is a long list that you do not want the audience to remember, such as a range of initiatives, products, reasons or actions. A long list gives an impression of plenty.

## Sonata

A sonata combines several musical phrases and develops them in three or four sections to make a musical whole. In speeches, too, we can combine many of the structures mentioned in this chapter to make more elaborate constructions. The longer the speech, the more structures it is likely to need.

## Structures that fall down

- **The 'elevator pitch'** This is the selling device that supposes you find yourself in a lift with someone you want to impress and have until the doors open to do so. You must start with your main point, then work back to the less important points before the doors open. It's a good technique for cutting waffle, and may work for the shortest speeches. However, because it puts the important points at the beginning and the least important at the end, there is no story so it makes a poor structure for a big speech.
- **The press-release format** An inverted pyramid, with the most important facts packed into the beginning and the less essential facts at the end. This makes it easy to read quickly, and if an editor needs to shorten the story, the loss of a few final words shouldn't damage the meaning. But it can make an unsatisfying speech, indigestible at the beginning and inconsequential by the end.

- **Tell them what you are going to tell them, tell them, tell them what you have told them** The advice given on many presentation-skills courses. But it doesn't give listeners what they want to hear. In any drama, novel, film or story, if the audience thinks the plot is too obvious, they switch off. A little mystery works wonders. What audiences seem to like best is to be able to follow a story easily, while hoping for a surprise. Give them a peek behind the curtain, but don't raise the whole curtain all at once.

### *Scrapheap Challenge:* dealing with contributions from different sources

*Scrapheap Challenge* is the bane of the speechwriter. Here, as in the TV programme, assorted junk has to be assembled into something that works. This is what happens when the speechwriter has to contend with contributions, in different formats and styles, on unrelated subjects, from colleagues who insist that the speech will be incomplete without them. The end result is still a load of old junk, no matter how carefully engineered. In any speech it is better to omit anything that the audience has no interest in hearing. If, as is sometimes unavoidable, some piecing together is required, ask the contributors to talk through what they want to say. Once someone has taken the trouble to put ideas on paper, they often become extremely difficult to destroy. But if the speechwriter produces a first draft, it can be changed without giving offence and the final version is likely to have more meaning.

### 'And finally'

All speeches need a 'philosophical, all-embracing conclusion'. To some extent it will depend on the introduction. If the speech began with a question, the conclusion should give the answer. If the speech began with the past and present, the conclusion should discuss the future. If the speech aims to be entertaining or thought-provoking, it should finish with a thought or moral for the audience to take away. If the speech promised a gift, now is the time to hand it over. The introduction and conclusion should make sense without the middle.

The place to end nearly all speeches is in the future, although when Charles Kennedy responded to the Hutton Inquiry in January 2004 he ended in the present:

> *Why was the decision to go to war at that point taken on the available information? Should not the United Nations weapons inspectorate have been given more time? Does not the case for an independent inquiry remain paramount? On 18 March 2003, this House debated an all-party amendment to which my party put all our names. It stated that the House 'believes that the case for war . . . has not yet been established'. The sad truth of the outcome of the Hutton inquiry is that as of today – nearly one year later – nothing fundamental has changed.*[21]

Only rarely should new material be introduced at the end of a speech. Ann Widdecombe, speaking in a debate on foxhunting in the House of Commons, 24 November 1997, kept back until the end of the speech a new analogy that became the most memorable section of the whole speech: 'The scenes of a hunt are splendid, so splendid that they are all over my dining-room curtains, but they are colourful scenes of olde England, and in olde England, not in modern Britain, they belong.' The House applauded, a rare event. Notice, too, the rhythm of the last sentence, like the blows of a hammer on a nail.

Simplicity may be preferable to unrealistic claims. Here is an example from President Bush's address to Congress after 11 September, and a similar broadcast by Osama Bin Laden:

> President Bush: *Freedom and fear, justice and cruelty have always been at war and we know that God is not neutral between them. Fellow citizens, we'll meet violence with patient justice – assured of the rightness of our cause, and confident of the victories to come. In all that lies before us, may God grant us wisdom, and may He watch over the United States of America.*[22]

> Osama Bin Laden: *I swear to God that America will not live in peace before peace reigns in Palestine, and before all the army of the infidels depart the land of Muhammad, peace be upon him. God is most great, and glory be to Islam.*[23]

Tony Blair concluded his 1999 Labour Party Conference speech in the paranoid tone that is noticeable in some of his major speeches:

> *The battleground, the new Millennium. Our values are our guide. Our job is to serve. Our workplace is the future. Let us step up the pace. Be confident. Be radical. To every nation a purpose. To every Party a cause. And now, at last, on the eve of the twenty-first century, Party and nation joined in the same cause for the same purpose: to set our people free.*[24]

It doesn't make sense, does it? Perhaps he was short of time. It does happen.

To conclude this section here is the peroration from King Edward VIII's abdication speech, delivered in 1936. When we compare the

King's draft with the final version we can see the improvements Winston Churchill made. The draft is heartfelt, speaks directly, and guides the listeners to their own reflections, but it ends with a note of uncertainty, and the choppy rhythm of the first, long, sentence would have been difficult to deliver.

> *Now that I have taken you fully into my confidence, as I have long wanted to, I feel it is best for me to go away for a while so that you may have time to reflect calmly and quietly but without undue delay on what I have said. Nothing is nearer to my heart than that I should return. But whatever may befall I shall always have a deep affection for my country and for all of you.*

The final version was:

> *I now quit altogether public affairs, and lay down my burden. It may be some time before I return to my native land, but I shall always follow the fortunes of the British race and Empire with profound interest, and if at any time in the future I can be found of service to His Majesty in a private station I will not fail. And now we have a new King. I wish him, and you, his people, happiness and prosperity with all my heart. God bless you all. God Save the King.*

# Three

# Words

Getting words on to paper is often regarded as the hardest part of writing a speech, but naturally effective speechmakers rely on certain 'trade secrets' that we can all learn to use – if we aren't already using them in ordinary conversation. If you enjoy writing, a speech gives you the chance to be creative and produce words fit for any occasion.

## Reducing the terror of the blank page

One of the questions most often put to me is how to start writing a speech. There seem to be two extreme approaches: one is to write something, anything, on the blank page and go from there; the other is to compose the entire speech in your head, then write it out. Only you know what works for you, and it is probably the way you approach any writing.

One way to get started is to leave your desk and switch off – walk the dog, dig the garden, go to the gym. Inspiration often makes its entrance when we are doing rather than thinking.

Another way is to learn some trade secrets and work around those.

## Trade secrets

Audiences are impressed by rhetoric, which is the art of persuasive speaking or writing. It is also associated with insincerity, exaggeration and brainwashing. There is nothing intrinsically wrong with speaking persuasively – we've probably done it effectively since we first persuaded a parent to buy an ice-cream. It is a basic human competence that develops throughout life. And we have probably all felt frustrated when someone has failed to persuade us with long-winded waffle or not plainly stated a request.

## Ten 'Claptraps'

In my experience of audience-watching, during speeches, sermons, lectures or comedy acts, the cues for response are certain sentences, phrases and words that are arranged in patterns known collectively as rhetorical devices or, because they can induce applause, 'claptraps'. They have probably been available to us since the first human beings used language. I'll introduce them with phrases from some 'classic' speeches as well as some more recent examples:

1. **Puzzle/solution** Elizabeth I presented a puzzle, 'I know I have the body of a weak and feeble woman . . .' and answered it, '. . . but I have the heart and stomach of a king, and a king of England too.'[1] The first half of a puzzle gains attention, the second half cues a response.
2. **Contrasts** 'One small step for a man, one giant leap for mankind' (Neil Armstrong).[2] 'Ask not what your country can do for you, but what you can do for your country' (John F. Kennedy).[3] The first half of a contrast gains attention; the second half cues a response.
3. **List of three** 'I came, I saw, I conquered' (Julius Caesar).[4] A list

of four may work, as in the next example where an extra point summarises the previous three: 'We shall fight on the beaches; we shall fight on the landing grounds; we shall fight in the fields and the streets; we shall fight in the hills; we shall never surrender.' (Winston Churchill).[5] Lists are countdowns or crescendos to applause, and work well in any series, especially time – past, present and future.

4. **Pictures with words** 'I have seen the promised land' (Martin Luther King).[6] Images make what is said more memorable. Abstract or real imagery can be used: journeys, buildings, nature, animals, space, sport, domestic routine, the human body, and time, are rich sources. An image may furnish a speech with a title by which it becomes known: Their Finest Hour,[7] Forces of Conservatism,[8] Axis of Evil.[9]

5. **Personal statements** 'An ideal for which I am prepared to die' (Nelson Mandela).[10] 'Non-violence is the first article of my faith, it is the last article of my faith.' (Mahatma Gandhi).[11] A personal statement may gain attention, cue applause and make what is said more memorable.

6. **Repetition** '... government of the people, by the people, for the people ... ' (Abraham Lincoln).[12] 'Education, education, education' (Tony Blair).[13] Alliteration is the repetition of the same letter or sound – 'Put up or shut up' (John Major).[14] Repetition and alliteration give emphasis to words and make what is said more memorable. They can be expanded: 'Tough on crime, tough on the causes of crime' (Tony Blair),[15] and developed, with a repetition of a word or phrase at the beginning of a sentence, such as in John Major's 'I want to see us build a country that is at ease with itself, a country that is confident, and a country that is prepared and willing to make the changes necessary to provide a better quality of life for all our citizens.'[16]

Or at the end: 'Gordon Brown promised pensioners change. They got it. Loose change.' (Michael Portillo).[17]

7. **Signposting** 'I have a dream' (Martin Luther King),[18] 'I warn you . . .' (Neil Kinnock),[19] 'Let me give you my vision' (Margaret Thatcher).[20] Signposts gain audience attention.

8. **Questions** 'I ask you, if women had had the vote, would we have had such laws?' (Emmeline Pankhurst).[21] 'A new dawn has broken has it not?' (Tony Blair).[22] 'Do not Iraqi women weep?' (Tony Benn).[23] Questions gain the audience's attention.

9. **Combinations of the above** On being sworn in as President of South Africa in 1994 Nelson Mandela used a list of three repetitive phrases, of which the third was itself a list of three: 'Let there be justice for all. Let there be peace for all. Let there be work for all. Let there be work, bread and salt for all.'[24] A puzzle can be followed with a contrast that provides the solution, or with a list – and so on. The combinations are endless. For example, to attract the listener's attention at the start of his 'Thought for the Day', on New Year's Day 2000, the Prince of Wales began with a puzzle, then a question combined with a list of three, in which each part of the list contained an image:

> *I suspect many of us will have been wondering how to approach the Millennium; wondering what it means in the midst of our daily lives. Will it – for instance – be an 'experience', the dawning of an exciting moment when we step boldly across the threshold marked 'Twenty-first Century' and emerge into the golden, promised land of a perennial future where there will be no more 'wailing and gnashing of teeth', where water flows uphill and the whole of humanity is genetically re-engineered.*[25]

10. **Stories, including jokes** These are in a league of their own (see page 55).

## Applause

A burst of applause is almost always preceded by lists, contrasts, puzzle/solutions and combinations of them all. The pattern of audience reaction was researched by Max Atkinson, and in his book *Our Masters' Voices*[26] he analysed political speeches from general elections of the 1980s which showed that:

1. Bursts of applause last for an average eight seconds, and vary from seven to nine seconds.
2. Both the speaker and the audience intervene to bring the applause to an end after eight seconds.
3. Only at the end of a speech is a burst of applause likely to last longer than eight seconds.
4. In the middle of a speech, bursts of applause longer than eight seconds are unusual but these are likely to be the sections reported by the media.
5. Audiences start to applaud just before a completion point, they know the clues for a completion point, they prepare themselves and start their applause in unison and exactly on cue.

If the speaker wants several bursts of applause, he or she must provide several completion points, the verbal cues to applause. An audience recognises a completion point mainly from the rhythm and form of the words spoken; volume, intonation and non-verbal cues play a lesser part. For example, the three-part list sounds solid and complete, and the last point has an air of finality that an audience readily recognises as a completion point. As soon as members of an audience realise a contrast is being delivered, they anticipate the second part of the contrast as the completion point. A speaker who knows these cues can use them to give advance warning that they expect applause and to indicate when it should start.

The lesson for speakers is clear: if a claptrap is to work, it has to build up in a series of distinct, recognisable phrases, as in 'On your marks, get set, go!'

An error in the way the 'claptrap' is constructed may confuse an audience: a contrast in which the second part doesn't echo the first, or a list that ends after only two items, or a puzzle with no obvious solution is likely to generate only feeble or sporadic applause, which can be worse than none at all. Worst of all is when the speaker expects applause but the audience doesn't and there is an embarrassing silence before the applause begins. The remedy is simple: make the completion points more obvious.

Of course what is said matters as much as how it is said, and Atkinson identified three types of message that are especially applaudable:

- Favourable references to persons
- Favourable references to 'us'
- Unfavourable references to 'them'.

In George Bush's 2004 State of the Union address, over twenty-five bursts of applause occurred after favourable reference to persons or America, such as, 'This great republic will lead the cause of freedom'; fifteen occur after unfavourable references to America's perceived enemies, such as, 'The once all-powerful ruler of Iraq was found in a hole, and now sits in a prison cell'; and some combined both, such as, 'The terrorists continue to plot against America and the civilised world, and by our will and courage, this danger will be defeated'.[27]

I would add a fourth type of applaudable message: the personal thoughts and feelings of the speaker. First, the audience wants to hear them, and second, they enhance the speaker's credibility. Someone who is lying cuts down on personal statements – they rarely use 'me' or 'I'. An audience listening to a speech with few or no personal statements may feel less inclined to believe what the speaker is saying. If you want your audience to trust you, identify with the statements you make.

Atkinson's research was made possible when video became widely available, allowing for detailed analysis – one minute of speech can take an hour to analyse – now we can all do it. At the next speech you hear live, observe the audience's responses. What form does it take? Attention gained, applause, laughter, silence? What words does the speaker use immediately before the response? Can you identify any rhetorical devices? With a video of a speech you can work out exactly when and for how long the audience applauded. Sometimes the analysis is possible without even being in the audience or seeing it on video or TV. It took only a few minutes to analyse George Bush's speech (above) because the White House obligingly publishes his speeches with the applause indicated on the transcript.

If rhetorical devices are so effective, why not use them all the time? First, because they magnify the meaning of the words and can produce unintentional effects. Second, because too many of them make the speech sound synthetic – as George Bush learned after the attacks on New York on 11 September 2001. He had been president for only a few months and was criticised for his poor performance in speeches. When he used a powerfully evocative puzzle and solution combined with a contrast, 'wanted, dead or alive', opinion was divided as to whether his Texas-ranch-style rhetoric showed he was in touch with America or out of his mind in an international world. In his speeches at this time he used a limited range of rhetorical devices, and those words seem more like a parody of a speech than a real one. In this sample each sentence is constructed from one of only five rhetorical devices:

*I will not settle for a token act.*

Abstract image

*Our response must be sweeping, sustained and effective.*

List of three

*We have much to do and much to ask of the American people.*

Repetition

*You will be asked for your patience: for, the conflict will not be short. You will be asked for resolve; for, the conflict will not be easy. You will be asked for your strength, because the course to victory may be long.*

Contrast combined with list of three [28]

It would have been an ordeal for any president to respond to the atrocities of 11 September, but Bush was new to the role and his speeches revealed a raw relationship with his speechwriters and a poor grasp of his own rhetoric. But he improved, and the discovery of a wider range of techniques to use in his speeches was one small part of that.

Surely it isn't that simple, though. Speakers don't select what they will say by choosing tools of rhetoric as though they were items on a menu, do they? Surely they don't sit down and say, 'I'll start with a puzzle, then a solution with a contrast. Then finish off with a nice list'? Well, I've never met anyone who worked like that. Gifted speakers use these devices automatically. Often they will write a first draft, then rework it for better effect, saving the most powerful devices for the important sections. This was what Gordon Brown did in his speech at the 2000 Labour Party Conference. In attacking shadow chancellor Michael Portillo's record, he used all ten rhetorical devices in one short section of his speech. It is based on a puzzle, posed in the form of a question 'Where was Portillo?', which he went on to solve. He repeated the formula four times:

> *And amidst all this economic mismanagement under the Tories is it not right that we ask, 'Where was Mr Portillo?' When it came to imposing VAT on fuel, is it not right that all of us ask, 'Where was Portillo?' I'll tell you where he was. At the Treasury, imposing VAT on fuel. When it came to imposing twenty-two Tory tax rises, is it not right that we all ask, 'Where was Portillo?' Well, I'll tell you. He was at the Treasury imposing every one of the twenty-two Tory tax rises. And just remember also, when it came to imposing the poll tax, is it not right that we all ask, 'Where was Portillo?' I'll tell you where he was. He was at the Department of the Environment, imposing the poll tax. And when it came to the biggest ever cuts in public spending and public services, is it not right that we also all ask, 'Where was Portillo?' I'll tell you where he was. At the Treasury imposing all of these cuts in public services.*[29]

The audience's attention was engaged by the question, to which in their own minds they worked out the answer and the range of scenarios – the imagery was implicit. Then Brown supplied the answers. The audience soon learned the formula, because the repetition made it predictable. By the third question they were reciting it in unison with the speaker and cheering after each answer. Their loudest and longest laughter was reserved for the final sentence – a puzzle with a solution that was a contrast to all that had gone previously: 'Of course, we all now know where Mr Hague was. He was on his fourteenth pint at the time.'

It was personal, authoritative, signposted, 'I'll tell you where he was …', alliterative – 'Twenty-two Tory tax rises'. The whole thing has a pantomime feel – entertaining, simple, formulaic, obvious, yet highly crafted and packed with rhetorical devices.

No analysis or method can substitute for the ability to say the right thing at the right time. Gifted speakers may deny they use these devices. On several occasions I have heard Tony Benn, a brilliant orator, dismiss them as rubbish. Yet we can see them in any of his speeches. Here he is in a speech about speeches:

> *To catch the speaker's eye is always a pleasure. To do it with the approval of the House of Commons is unheard of* [repetition with a contrast]. *I take this award as the rehabilitation of the speech, the full speech, as a part of the political process* [personal statement, signpost]. *A speech is not like a book. You don't know who's going to read a book or when or why* [two contrasts, list of three]. *A speech is a process relating the speaker, the subject, the audience, the time and the place* [list]. *And for my part my views have been made of my experience and what I've heard* [personal, signpost]. *I've never been influenced by a soundbite, by a pager message, by a poll, by a focus group, by a scriptwriter* [first part of contrast combined with a list]. *Always by listening to people and learning* [second part of contrast]. *And we live in difficult times when the level of political debate is often shallow, personalised and abusive* [first part of contrast with list of three]. *Whereas the problems are challenging, interesting and difficult* [second part of

contrast with list of three]. *And we need the right of free speech coupled with the right to be heard* [repetition].[30]

Benn used a device in every sentence. And all off-the-cuff. A few weeks later he gave an almost identical speech. And that's the thing with experienced speakers: they are not as 'off-the-cuff' as they appear. Their magic is thoroughly rehearsed.

For a busy speaker, though, there isn't time to craft every speech to the same standard, in most speeches the packaging is less than perfect. For example, Tony Blair flew to Johannesburg for the 2002 Earth Summit. Most of the preparations were focused on the main speech for the following day. On the day he arrived he gave another speech:[31] 'What is truly shocking is not the scale of the problems, the truly shocking thing is that we know the remedies. Where the wealthy countries have acted it has made a difference. It is not rocket science, it is a matter of political will and leadership.'[31] In this extract two imperfectly packaged contrasts sandwich a sentence that doesn't quite fit. The second part of the contrast at the end sounds as if it is heading for a list of three but stops after two. The audience waited for the third part of the list, which never came. There was an awkward gap before they applauded dutifully. The day after, in his main speech, he simplified the conclusion to better effect: 'We know the problems. We know the solutions. Together, as one world, we must find the will to deliver them.'

Some devices become trademarks of the speakers who use them. Tony Blair often starts with a negative in the first part of a contrast in which both parts are a list of three, as in this typical statement of intent from his speech outside 10 Downing Street on 2 May 1997: 'This was not a mandate for dogma or doctrine or a return to the past. But it was a mandate to get those things done in our country that desperately need doing for the future of Britain.'

Once you are familiar with the techniques in this chapter, you will hear and see them all around you; they are the devices of advertising, headlines and the media quote. In the decades after the war, it seemed that every marketable commodity had an advertising slogan that relied on alliteration, 'Guinness is good for you', 'For mash get Smash', 'Beanz Meanz Heinz', or combined with an image, 'Polo, the mint with the hole'. Then there were lists; the 'Snap, crackle and pop' for Rice Krispies, and 'A Mars a day helps you work, rest and play'. There were puzzles in 'Go to work on an egg', or 'Use your loaf'. No wonder such phrases became known as 'soundbites'. They are beloved of headline writers – and not just the tabloids. A recent edition of the *Daily Telegraph*[32] includes contrast in 'Microsoft Founder fined a very small fortune', alliteration in 'Virus sends coastguard computer off course,' and an intriguing image, 'Clinton skips over Monica'.

We use these devices in everyday conversation, especially when expressing emotion. In love or anger we often express ourselves in images: we 'say it with flowers'. In swearing, you may use alliteration with b, f, sh – the same powerful consonants and sounds that Churchill used in the speech quoted on page 43.

We don't really know how the devices work. Bill Clinton touched on why some messages are especially applaudable in his explanation of 'us and them' in his speech to the Labour Party Conference in 2002:

> *Since humanity came out of Africa aeons ago, the whole history of our species has been marked by human beings' attempts to meet their needs and fulfil their hopes, confront their dangers and fears, through both conflict and co-operation. We have come to define the meaning of our lives in relationship to other people. We derive positive meanings through positive associa-tions with our groups and we give ourselves importance also by*

*negative reference to those who are not part of 'us'. There has*
*never been a person – I do not think of any age, and I bet it*
*applies to everyone in this room – who has not said at least*
*once in your life if not out loud, 'Well, I may not be perfect but*
*thank God I am not one of them.' That basically has been the*
*pattern of life.*[33]

The word patterns work in the same mysterious way as music or poetry: the same rhythms have the same effect – the two-time rhythm of contrasts, the three notes of a series that form a harmonic chord, the repetition and alliteration that provide emphasis like repeated notes in music.

Rhetorical devices, whatever their ingredients, are powerful, and they magnify the meaning of whatever is said. This can lead to some unintended effects. Maybe Iain Duncan Smith's 'quiet man' epithet would not be the only remembered phrase of his lengthy speech at the 2002 Conservative Party Conference if it hadn't been so over-packaged. It started with a signpost combined with a puzzle, which was answered by a list of three, with repetition at both the beginning and the end of each part of the list: 'Those who do not know me yet will come to understand this: When I say a thing, I mean it. When I set myself a task, I do it. When I settle on a course, I stick to it. Do not underestimate the determination of a quiet man.'[34] The applause lasted almost a minute, far longer than would have been expected, which would confirm reports that 'plants' were in the audience to prolong it artificially.

The best-remembered passage from one of John Major's speeches – 'Fifty years on from now, Britain will still be the country of long shadows on county [cricket] grounds, warm beer, invincible green suburbs, dog lovers and old maids bicycling to Holy Communion through the morning mist'[35] – is constructed of a signpost, followed by a list packed with three images. It became a caricature of his political philosophy.

Foreign Office officials might have spared the Queen a heckling during a speech in Ghana in 1999 if they had used a tool of rhetoric more carefully.[36] 'Next year your president who has led you through momentous changes, will reach the end of his second term' said the Queen. It was a puzzle to an audience that was divided as to whether the end of President Rawlings' term of office was a good or bad prospect. They rumbled, laughed and booed. The Queen looked unsure. Eventually she continued: 'His successor is to be chosen freely and fairly by the people of Ghana. This election will itself demonstrate the political change and freedom which Ghana now enjoys.' The image of improved democracy should have come first, not last in a back-to-front time series.

### The tools are in whatever you want to say

If we look at the content of what we want to say, we invariably find that our material is made of contrasts, puzzles, lists, personal statements, etc. A speech for a retirement party might include:

- Contrasts: between work and retirement, between then and now
- Puzzles: what will he/she do with their time?
- Lists: achievements, thanks
- Personal statements: recollections of the speaker about the person retiring.

You could probably pick any policy or strategy you are involved with in your own area of business or politics and write a sentence or two to express it as a contrast, a list of three, a personal statement or a puzzle/solution.

Those who take the view that the devices and techniques mentioned in this section are the language of propaganda and should be avoided are left with a problem: what methods should they use to craft their speech? What is left if the techniques in this chapter are taken away? If a speaker wants to convey truth, passion or sincerity, or to convince someone legitimately of their case or to speak on behalf of another, how can they do it if these devices are denied to them? The options seem limited.

### Stories, including humour

Stories and humour make a speech more enjoyable, interesting and entertaining for speaker and listener. To include them in a speech:

- Draw from material with which the speaker will be familiar – avoid anything that might sound phoney.
- Use stories that reinforce the message. In a speech at the Institute of Directors I heard the rhyme 'You shake and shake and shake the bottle, First none'll come and then the lot'll' used as a warning of the effects of the EU Social Chapter on regulations for British business.
- Consider the audience. The rhyme I have just quoted may not be clear to an audience of non-English speakers.

Here is a piece of old advice I've found useful: 'All anecdotes are ornaments: some are like bangles that can be slipped on and off, others are like brooches that, sparkling themselves, hold other things together. These are really the only anecdotes worthwhile.'[37]

In general, avoid foreign words or phrases. Did the Queen gain more than she lost when, in November 1992, she started her speech at the Lord Mayor's banquet: 'Nineteen ninety-two is not a year I shall look back on with undiluted pleasure. In the words of one of my more sympathetic correspondents, it has turned out to be an "Annus Horribilis".'?[38] Jokes, quotations and certain figures of speech, including some rhetorical devices, do not translate well from English to other languages. During the war in Afghanistan, George Bush talked about 'smoking out' terrorists, which was translated into Arabic as meaning that the US would use chemical weapons.[39] And humour should never offend: you could lose your audience – or your job, as shadow rural-affairs minister Ann Winterton discovered after making a racist joke to a rugby club audience in May 2002.

Self-effacing humour nearly always works. William Hague was speaking off-the-cuff in Blackpool at the 2001 Conservative Party Conference, soon after he had lost the leadership, when he said, 'Once I gave a speech in this hall when I said half of you won't be here in thirty years time but I will be. [Laughter] I was wrong, twenty-four years on you're still here and I've been and gone. [More laughter]'[40] The device? A double contrast with figures.

Some people have what I once heard a clergyman call a 'gatherum omnium' for their clippings and stories, but don't waste time searching joke books – they'll be the wrong sort of jokes. Find your own humour in your material. Audiences like speakers with a sense of humour. If you can see the funny side of life, humour will arise naturally from your subject. To find humour, look for incongruity and mismatches. Incongruity lends itself to the rhetorical device of contrast, in which the first half is the 'normal' and the second part 'incongruous'. The audience goes along with the speaker, not expecting anything unusual, then suddenly the incongruity pops up. That and the surprise provoke the laughter. The Queen seldom uses humour in her speeches, but she was in good form during the Golden Jubilee celebrations in 2002, which coincided with the World Cup. After lunch at the Guildhall, she started predictably:

'My Lord Mayor, Prime Minister, ladies and gentlemen, thank you, my Lord Mayor, for your invitation for lunch at Guildhall today. It is a great pleasure once again for Prince Philip and me to be in this historic building to add another anniversary celebration to its long record of national events.' [Then] 'I am aware at the moment of the interest in football.' A split second of silence was followed by a guffaw as the audience realised they had been caught off-guard. She went on: 'As far as we are concerned it bears no relation to a rest at half-time.'[41] The audience responded with more laughter and a round of applause. It was self-effacing, personal, topical, and it worked. Had she said, 'My Golden Jubilee takes place in the middle of the World Cup. This weekend is rather like the break at half-time' it would have raised no more than a smile. And in another Golden Jubilee speech, when Prince Charles incongruously addressed the Queen as 'Your Majesty, Mummy' the audience cheered.

### Writing the spoken word

One of the commonest criticisms I hear from those who have speeches prepared for them is that the drafts they are given don't sound like spoken English. Most of us communicate effectively in speech. We learn to do so in our first four years. The human brain is unmatched as a decoding machine for the spoken word, and we use it for this purpose long before we can speak. However, the ear takes a string of words one at a time. Max Atkinson suggested the reason most bursts of applause are eight seconds long might be to do with short-term memory: when eight seconds has elapsed the audience has forgotten what prompted them to applaud.[42] It is a daunting challenge for a speaker to provide something of interest every eight seconds, and to structure words for speech. The tables that follow offer guidelines that may be helpful in writing the spoken word.

## Writing the spoken word

1. **Speak while you write** And keep reading aloud, preferably to someone else.

2. **Imagine the speaker's voice in your head** – your own or that of the person you are writing for. Watch your speaker in action, live or on video, ask their colleagues about their speech mannerisms; talk to them informally. Some speakers have difficulty pronouncing certain consonants: if this is so, keep it in mind.

3. **Imagine you are talking one-to-one with a friend over a drink in the pub** Many people find this a good way to write down clearly what they mean and dispense with jargon.

4. **Think poetry** Does the writing have the flow and rhythm of verse? If not, change it.

5. **Think 'one chance'** A listener has only one chance to hear and understand, so simple sentences work best. Include 'fillers': 'you see', 'you know', 'I mean'. They summarise, justify, soften, explain and mark boundaries, slow the pace and allow time for understanding.

6. **Structure the speech clearly** All listeners like to hear a good story. Anticipate the audience reaction. Read the speech to yourself and ask yourself, What am I thinking at this point? What do I want to know next?

7. **Spell out acronyms** Reduce them to the minimum, but if you have to include them, spell them out in full at the first appearance.

8. **Don't worry about grammar** Write as you speak and it will be fine. See also pages 62 and 161.

9. **Be wary of weird words** – See page 59.

10. **Say something interesting at least every eight seconds** Listeners are easily bored.

## Weird words to be wary of

1.  **Homonyms** Words with two different meanings: affair, arm(s), capital, coach, chip, country, economy, field, firm, good, key, march, may, premise(s), second, train.

2.  **Homographs** Words of the same spelling where the meaning is clear only in the pronunciation: minute, wind, produce, lead, conduct, wound.

3.  **Homophones** Words that sound alike but have two or more different spellings and meanings. A reader can see the word and will know the intended meaning, but a listener may get the wrong idea. The examples that follow include some words that are not strictly homophones but where accurate pronunciation is necessary for the listener to distinguish the meaning.

| | | |
|---|---|---|
| accept/except | cue/queue | red/read |
| affect/effect | draft/draught | right/write |
| air/heir | eight/ate | see/sea |
| already/all ready | ensure/insure | sight/site |
| altogether/all together | fair/fare | sun/son |
| biannual/biennial | four/for | tale/tail |
| board/bored | great/grate | taught/taut |
| bold/bowled | hole/whole | tide/tied |
| born/borne | hour/our | their/there |
| canvas/canvass | lesson/lessen | two/to/too |
| cash/cache | mail/male | weigh/way |
| cell/sell | not/knot | weak/week |
| council/counsel | one/won | wear/where |
| course/coarse | peace/piece | world/whirled |
| | pole/poll | |

4. **Oronyms** Strings of sound that the ear can divide into more than one group of words: 'stuff he knows' or 'stuffy nose'.

5. **Tongue twisters** If you are encumbered with a phrase such as post-legislative scrutiny, Water Framework Directive, weapons of mass destruction, Slobodan Milosevic or the Human Fertilisation and Embryology Authority, treat it like jumps in a steeplechase: make sure the approach and landing are flat, with simple words on either side.

6. **Cultural difference.** A reminder of a few differences in vocabulary if you are British writing for an American audience or vice versa.

| American | British |
| --- | --- |
| administration | government |
| auto | car |
| first floor | ground floor |
| math | maths |
| line | queue |
| lawyer | solicitor |
| fall | autumn |
| mentor | tutor |
| pants | trousers |

### Where written material is the starting point

1.  **Sum up the main message**  Read the written material and find a way to sum up what you want to say in one sentence. The audience will want to know the principal general point. It may be all they remember: they will not retain a mass of detail.

2.  **Write spoken English,** which does not necessarily mean sentences, but short phrases. Use the present tense, plenty of verbs, few nouns.

3.  **Take out the headings**  A speech has none.

4.  **Use verbal signposts** to replace visual ones.

5.  **Avoid bullet points**  They don't work in a speech as the listener loses the thread. Keep any lists simple: indicate at the beginning what it is about and use 'First . . .', 'Second . . .' and 'Finally . . .' to keep the listener on track. If there are more than three points in a list, subdivide it.

6.  **Keep punctuation to a minimum**

7.  **Create soundbites** so that the big ideas are simply expressed and long remembered.

8.  **Quotations** Ensure the listener knows when they begin and end.

9.  **Lay out the speech as a script** see pages 161-169.

10. **The 'afterlife'** . . . A speech may have an afterlife as a press release or an article. After it has been delivered, put in some headings, any sources of reference, number lists, etc., to produce a version suitable for publication.

**Just enough grammar**

1. All a sentence needs is a verb and a noun: 'Time passes'; 'Ministers decide'; 'Love hurts'. Concentrate on good nouns and verbs and you are halfway there. Keep the verb close to the noun.

2. Verbs give life to a sentence, so choose carefully.

3. Where possible, use the active, not the passive mood with the verb so that the subject of the sentence is doing something: 'The manager sacked the cleaners', rather than 'The cleaners were sacked'. Save the passive for sentences like 'The five economic tests can be met'; 'The details are set out in the Treasury memorandum'.

4. Maintain the present tense.

5. Use 'we' rather than 'you'.

6. Avoid the split infinitive, though 'To go boldly' wouldn't give the same ring to the preface to *Startrek*. 'Space, the final frontier. These are the voyages of the starship Enterprise. It's five year mission: to explore strange new worlds, to seek out new life and new civilisations, to boldy go where no man has gone before.'[43] 'Boldly to go' might be better still.

## Dealing with figures

Major speeches often involve figures: transform them into a manageable scale in relation to something familiar, such as per person, per family, per week. A Northern Ireland sports minister made this point: 'The sum total of our subsidy to sport comes to about 25 pence per person per week – the price of a packet of crisps!'[44] Lists and contrasts work just as well with figures as with words. A big figure only works when it means something: if you must use one, round it to the nearest million or billion.

Captain Mike Bannister used mostly numbers combined with graphic images to capture the drama of Concorde's last flight (24 October 2003):

> *We are going to take you to the edge of space. Where the sky gets darker. Where you can see the curvature of the earth. We are going to travel across the Atlantic at twice the speed of sound. Faster than a rifle bullet. Twenty-three miles every minute. We are going to travel so fast . . . faster than the earth rotates. And the world will be watching us.*

### Dealing with quotations

Make clear the start and end of a quotation. Here an example is woven into a conference speech:

> *But the real find came a little later on. A handwritten letter from Sawrey, Ambleside, dated the eighth of November 1939, and I wonder if you can guess its author? 'Dear Sir,' it starts, 'I have had an unexpected cheque for seventy pound fourteen shillings for an infringement of copyright' – another clue there. 'I had been thinking when I read your last report (also when I was ill in hospital) what a fine idea that is of special training in practical work for young architects – May I give seventy pounds anonymously to the fund? It is a misfortune – a perplexing minor tragedy – that experience goes out like the snuff of a candle. The young are apt to think us old ones conceited – and the old ones apt to think the same of the younger generation.' There's a little bit more and she signs off 'I remain Sir, yours sincerely, H. B. Heelis.' She was, of course, Beatrix Potter.*[45]

Only the phrase 'another clue there' depends on the speaker's delivery to be understood.

On the whole, though, unless you have a real 'find' like the one above, don't use quotations in a speech. It is better to make new ones. Say it yourself and let other people quote you.

### Spontaneous or prepared?

The spoken word may not look good on paper. Michael Caine's Oscar-acceptance speech in March 2000 was one of the best of the evening, yet my transcript is barely comprehensible:

> *Thank you. I was looking watching all the others and thinking back when I saw the performances. I'm thinking of how the Academy changed 'the winner is' to 'the Oscar goes to', and if ever there was a category where the Oscar goes to someone without there being a winner, it's this one, because I do not feel like being the winner. You have Michael, who I'd never heard of, quite frankly, who is astonishing. You have Jude, who is going to be a big star no matter what happens. You have Tom, who, if you had won this, your price would have gone down so fast. Have you any idea what supporting actors get paid? And we only get one motorhome. A small one . . .*

He changes thought mid-sentence. He doesn't complete every sentence. It's not all grammatically correct. It is disjointed, like a real conversation. The speech worked because it sounded like Michael Caine, spontaneous, restless, risky. It is, of course, hard to make a prepared draft sound as spontaneous as the one above.

Sometimes a speech must work as both written and spoken word, like a well-crafted essay. Big speeches are nearly always better as essays: copies are distributed, possibly in advance, and if the speech is important, journalists and commentators will read, then analyse what was said. Every line becomes subject to scrutiny.

## Clichés

The usual advice on clichés is to avoid them, but they are too close to proverb and metaphor to be dismissed. Also, because they are familiar, they will be grasped by a wide audience. They can be powerful: Margaret Thatcher took the play title The Lady's Not for Burning, changed a letter, and 'The lady's not for turning' became the best-remembered sentence of her career.[46]

It is when clichés are used without thought that they sound worn out. 'At the end of the day' was once a perfectly good phrase, alluding, perhaps, to what we set most store by. It became cliché when misused as a way of foreshortening discussion with a simplistic assumption. All sorts of proverbs, idiom, quotations, words, figures of speech can be given a twist to take on a new lease of life (there's one!), reflect a new truth and make it matter.

Play around with any of these to update them:

- Cut and run
- You can't have your cake and eat it
- Every dog has his day
- Whitewash
- The hare and the tortoise
- How long is a piece of string?
- He who hesitates is lost
- Look before you leap
- A stitch in time saves nine
- The road less travelled

- At the end of the day
- They're changing guard at Buckingham Palace
- The business of America is Business
- Winning the battle but losing the war
- A nation of shopkeepers
- Death is the great leveller.

Laurence Llewelyn-Bowen experimented with the last two: 'So it seems MDF, not death, is the great leveller. The standard of design literacy is so high that, rather than a nation of shopkeepers, we have become a nation of interior designers.' [47]

## Jargon

Jargon is an organisation's own language, and a speaker uses it to indentify themselves with the 'club' to which the jargon is unique. The problem is not that the audience won't understand – though there will invariably be someone who hears it for the first time – but that becomes a substitute for thought-through ideas. Also, once someone has learnt it, they may forget what it means.

Worse, it can obscure meaning. Nowhere is that more chilling than in speeches of war: 'neutralise', 'friendly fire' and 'collateral damage' mean that people have been killed.

Beyond jargon comes gobbledegook. One form is a hybrid of management- and mandarin-speak. It is easy to learn – new civil servants pick it up in weeks – but it is almost meaningless. The National Health Service suffers from more than its fair share: here are some extracts from a speech by former health secretary Alan Milburn.

*Over the next few years all parts of the NHS must be reformed, redesigned around the needs of patients. Earlier this year I set out in a speech how reform must fundamentally change the relationship between patients and the service. I said then that patients should have more information, more influence and more power over the services they receive. I called for the balance of power in the NHS to shift decisively in favour of the patient.*

*The new strategic health authorities will be the bridge between the Department of Health and local NHS services. They will have an absolutely crucial role to play in brokering solutions to local problems, holding local health services to account and encouraging greater autonomy for NHS Trusts and PCTs. They will need to be well run, highly efficient organisations attracting some of the best management. So I can say today that I am examining proposals for ensuring this happens including inviting expressions of interest from the best performing management teams to run the strategic health authority 'franchise'.*[48]

Perhaps the best way to learn how to avoid gobbledegook is to be aware of how it is constructed:

- It is full of clichés.
- It has plenty of words.
- It uses negatives.
- It avoids repetition or rhythm.
- It uses context-specific vocabulary, or everyday words that have a different meaning in the specific sense.
- It uses abstract concepts with no examples.
- It is laced with adjectival nouns.

- It uses the passive mood.
- Nothing is in the first person.
- Each sentence is the same length.
- It refers to the past and future, never now, and mixes up the sequence of time.
- It distances the content from real life by referring to people only by their titles, not names, or as collective groups, such as 'the public'.

When the Plain English Campaign compiled its list of Britain's most-loathed clichés, Tony Benn wove them all together in a letter to *The Times*:

> *The important thing is that we clarify the bottom line as set out in the mission statement that we have put out for consultation with a view to developing a network from which the final analysis can be brought into the calculation at the end of the day, guaranteeing diversity and environmentally acceptable policies for the community, protecting vulnerable people by modernising and reforming so as to move the goal posts and bring about a level playing field and actually involve naming and shaming those who are seeking to frustrate the outcome which must involve seeing Britain at the heart of Europe, with a special relationship as the basis of the coalition of the willing to bring about regime change in the rest of the world that will secure social responsibility and facing the reality that there are tough choices to be made and the buck stops with us as there is no easy option.*[49]

## Changing pace and direction

A little mystery and/or drama help; too much and a speech will sound like a rant. It is worth reading through a speech to check its pace, light and shade. Assess how fast or slow it is: is it a plod or a gallop? Try to make it sound sprightly. A speech sounds slow if too much is in the past tense, and if it is all theory. To speed it up, alternate between the universal and the particular, and make sure the natural rhythm of the words is fast. To slow a speech down, introduce pauses for thought, and filler expressions such as 'I see', 'you know', 'I mean'.

## The words on paper

The process of writing can be long. As people progress in their careers, they spend more rather than less time on their speeches. Many junior ministers give a lot of small speeches, on minor occasions, spending little time on each – not always to best effect for them or their audiences – but the time comes when they fail to prepare adequately and a speech goes so badly that they wonder what went wrong. From this point they prepare thoroughly and spend more time on the writing. The more important your role, the more likely it is that you will need to speak verbatim from a full draft and to have a script available for journalists, commentators and others. Use the tools of rhetoric to elicit the reactions you want from your audiences. Do not overlook your imagination: the tools, techniques and methods mentioned in this chapter merely package it.

*Four*

# Special occasions

A speech is part of the ritual of a special occasion, transforming the audience from individuals to a group, creating a sense of unity and capturing the mood of the moment. Imagine you are launching a ship. Perhaps you would say, as the Queen did in January 2004, 'I name this ship Queen Mary Two. God bless her and all who sail in her.' Then crack a bottle of champagne over the bows. You would know exactly what to say and do, though most of us have not and never will launch a ship. Yet people struggle with more routine occasions and at family gatherings – weddings and funerals especially. Bigger speeches – at debates or conferences – are a challenge even for the expert speaker.

In this chapter I suggest some time-saving formulas for dealing with making introductions, offering a vote of thanks, presenting and accepting awards, visits, toasts, after-dinner speaking, tributes, appeals, media interviews and candidacy speeches – in other words, how to 'say a few words'. We will look at how to bring wedding speeches up to date, and how to make a funeral oration, then go on to look at debates, conferences, lectures and parliamentary speeches.

## 'Say a few words'

An impromptu speech can induce paralysis because the speaker doesn't know what to say. The best preparation is to think about it beforehand.

Research is useful, but it is better to identify what you feel about the occasion then put it into words. Ask yourself three questions:

1. What are you enjoying about being here?
2. What can you say that is sincere, true and important to all the audience?
3. What must you do for the audience? Welcome them, thank them, say goodbye to them or make a toast? Unveil a plaque, present an award or crack a bottle of champagne over the bows?

How do you decide what is sincere, true and interesting to you and the audience? Some people have a 'nose' for the mood and opinions of their audience. The rest of us may find it helps to think of a strong image, make it the theme and link everything around it. It presents the audience with a puzzle to which the rest of the speech becomes the solution.

For example, a flower provided the theme of John Clark's address to the Women's Institute in the film *Calendar Girls*.

> *The flowers of Yorkshire are like the women of Yorkshire – every stage of their growth has its own beauty. But the last phase is the most glorious. Then very quickly they all go to seed. Which makes it ironic: my favourite flower isn't even indigenous to the British Isles, let alone Yorkshire. I don't think there is anything on this planet that more trumpets life than the sunflower. For me, that's because of the reason behind its name. Not because it looks like the sun, but because it follows the sun. During the course of the day the head tracks the journey of the sun across the sky. A satellite dish for sunshine. Wherever the light is, no matter how weak, these flowers will find it. And that's such an admirable thing. And such a lesson in life.*[1]

Another easy option is to say something about the present, the past and the future: Where are we now? How did we get here? Where are we going?

Answering three interesting questions is perhaps the most useful and easiest way of considering what to put into a speech. Suppose you are a film actor who has been nominated for an Oscar and you are planning an acceptance speech. Interesting questions might be:

1. How do you feel accepting the Oscar?
2. What was it like working with the director/leading actress?
3. Who inspired you?
4. How did you prepare for the part?
5. What does it mean to you to win the Oscar?
6. What will you do with your Oscar?
7. What moral did you take from the film?
8. What message do you have for junior actors?
9. Is there a wider social comment about the film?
10. What will you do next?

You don't want to answer all ten because it is a short speech and you won't remember ten points: choose the three most interesting ones. This formula is especially useful if you are coaching someone else for a speech. Ask them some questions, let them reply off the cuff and suggest that the most interesting replies form the basis of their speech.

On his release in 1991 Terry Waite's moving extempore speech answered the questions the world had been unable to ask him during his five years as a hostage in Beirut. He recalled[2] that the speech was crafted on the plane to RAF Lyneham. It had been suggested that he might 'want to say a word or two' to 'one or two' members of the press. He borrowed a pen and jotted down a few notes on the back of an envelope. At Lyneham he was driven to a hangar where a large crowd of journalists and supporters waited. His first words spoke of his feelings about the occasion as if to a group of friends: 'Ladies and gentlemen, I think you can imagine that after 1763 days in chains it's an overwhelming experience to come back and receive your greetings.' He went on to address the following questions: Who should be thanked? What has happened to Terry Anderson, the hostage still in Beirut? What is my message to my captors? What helped keep me alive? This is an extract:

> *And one day, out of the blue, a guard came into my room with a postcard, it was a postcard of the stained glass window from Bedford showing John Bunyan in jail, and I looked at that card and I thought, My word, Bunyan, you're a lucky fellow, you've got a window out of which you can look and see the sky and here I am in a dark room; you've got pen and ink and you can write and I've got nothing; and you've got your own clothes and a table and chair; and I turned the card over and there was a message from someone whom I didn't know simply saying, 'We remember, we shall not forget, we shall continue to work for the people who are detained around the world.' I can tell you all, that thought brought me back to the marvellous work of agencies like Amnesty International and their letter-writing campaigns. I would say to you all, never despise those simple actions. Something, somewhere will get through to the people you are concerned about, as it got through to me and my fellow hostages eventually.*

The purpose of his speech – to satisfy immediate media interest and thus provide himself with privacy to meet his family – came through in his concluding remarks:

*Enough for the moment. Once again my gratitude to you, my thanks to you, and I hope that I shall have the opportunity at a later date of speaking in greater detail and perhaps a little more personally. Thank you.*[3]

It was an extraordinary performance, all the more so because he had reminded us earlier in his speech that 'I was kept in total and complete isolation for four years. I saw no one and spoke to no one apart from a cursory word with my guards when they brought me food.'

But for most of us, most of the time, a sentence or two can be enough. 'It's been a great joy to me. The marchers, the children, my regiments and especially the music . . . have all been a joy', followed by a smile and a wave was the entire speech the Queen Mother gave to conclude her hundredth-birthday pageant.

Experienced speakers are always ready with off-the-cuff remarks. Generally they have prepared them well in advance, committed them to memory or a slip of paper. Many an after-dinner speech has been mapped out on a table napkin. For a formal occasion, have with you a separate list of names and correct forms of address, in the right order, and glance at them before you speak.

For practice and for leadership, it is worth mastering how to 'say a few words'. You might want to think ahead to the occasions coming up where you might need to do so and prepare a few ideas in readiness.

### Introducing a speaker

Introducing an occasion's principal speaker is a good opportunity to practice speechmaking: you can bring the audience together, set the tone of the event and generate interest in the speaker. Both audience and speaker will be grateful to you, and you will establish your own credibility. But 'No speech is more mangled than the speech of introduction, probably because it is looked on as unimportant' lamented Dale Carnegie, ninety years ago in his classic textbook of public speaking,[4] and the same is true today.

The mnemonic T-I-P may help you shape your introduction:

T = Topic: what's the speaker's topic?
I = Importance: why is the subject important and interesting?
P = Person: who is the speaker? Why are they outstanding in their field?

Puzzles/solutions, stories, signposts and personal statements (see chapter 3, pages 42-45) are useful devices in generating interest. The effect of the introduction should be sincere and short. If you want a round of applause, bring in the speaker's name at the last moment: 'Please join me now in welcoming to the platform our special guest, [name].'

If you are the main speaker, should someone introduce you? One school of thought maintains that it is better to introduce yourself because then no one else has the chance to mess it up. Another says that someone else should introduce you because they can be flattering, create interest in you and generally warm up the audience. It's a matter of judgement, depending on who is likely to make the introduction. Decide whether you will leave the preparation to the introducer, suggest a few points they might include or give them a prepared draft.

## Thanking a speaker, and other votes of thanks

At the minimum, all you need is to complete three sentences along the lines of:

1. 'We've been pleased/honoured to have you to speak to us . . .'
2. 'It was interesting/fascinating/funny because . . .'
3. 'We wish you well/success in . . .'

## Presenting awards

This is a pleasant task, but not always done well. Consider the scenario: the guest speaker has a card with the winner's name. He or she looks at it and reads: 'The winner is Mary Lancaster.' A few people clap but there is no sign of Mary making her way to the platform. The speaker tries again: 'Mary wins this year's gold medal.' There's another ripple of applause, and someone who might be Mary hovers uncertainly by the platform, so the speaker says, 'I'd like to present the medal now to Mary.' Mary is confused and so is the audience, some of whom applaud after 'Lancaster', some after 'medal'. By the time Mary is on the stage they have stopped clapping and the presentation takes place in an awkward silence.

Cue the audience to applaud by mentioning the winner's name last: 'I'd like to present the medal now to the winner. In first place, the winner of this year's gold medal is . . . Mary Lancaster.' All the audience will applaud as Mary bounds on to the platform.

Combine this technique with another rhetorical device: the build-up is improved and the applause will be louder and longer. A signpost is already there, 'I'd like to present the medal now to the winner', to which could be added a list of three: 'And in first place, with the highest marks we've seen in five years, the winner is Mary Lancaster.' Know what you are presenting – a nice gesture is to show it to the audience before you present it.

## Accepting an award

Your first task is to accept the award, then decide quickly what you are going to do with it – unwrap it, hold it aloft, give it someone else to hold? Unless you've won the booby prize, you must appear to be sincere and look pleased: smile, thank the person who has presented you with the award, then turn to the audience and make a short speech. If you need to say more than thank you, some questions in the table on page 88 may help you decide what to say. If you must thank a lot of people, have their names ready. The humourist Matthew Parris accepted an award with a single sentence of thanks structured as a list:

> *To my dear secretary Eileen, who photocopies Alan Coren's articles, and gives them to me saying, 'Now that's what I call humour', to the Members of both Houses on whose discomfort I have fed for thirteen years and whom I have too often forgotten do feel pain as ordinary humans do, to William Hague, about whom I have been perfectly horrid for years and years and who in response has never been anything but really nice to me, and to Channel 4, thank you very much.[5]*

## Visits

The speech for a visit to an office, hospital, school or factory should be short because the audience is invariably standing. It is not the occasion for drawn-out statements of policy, but there is still plenty to say. The following mnemonic will guide you though the preparations:

V  = Venue: what is the significance of the venue?
I  = 'I . . .': what are you enjoying about being here?
S  = Staff: what can you say that is sincere and true about them?
I  = Importance: why is the occasion important?
T  = Thanks: who do you need to thank and what for?
     and/or Thought to Take Away: what thought can you leave with the audience?

You can make the points in any order. It helps to have seen round the venue before you speak: you will have first-hand experience to draw on.

## Toasts

Proposing a toast is a small act of social leadership that turns any gathering into a celebration and an audience enjoys getting it right. They like to have their glasses ready, raise them and repeat the words of the toast in unison. So, if you are proposing the toast you must provide the right cues, signal the actions and say a few words.

First of all, find the right moment to stand and say, 'I would like to propose a toast to X.' For a bigger gathering you may need to say more: 'Ladies and gentlemen, let's raise our glasses to the success of X/ future of X/ health of X/ to X', or even to preface it with something like 'In a moment I would like to propose a toast to . . . So if you would all have your glasses ready . . .'

Lift your glass slowly to shoulder height – the guests will obligingly follow your actions – and as you get to 'to X' look in X's direction.

In Britain, the Loyal Toast, the traditional signal for the end of a meal and the start of smoking, is rarely made any more. If you are required to propose the Loyal Toast a speech is neither required nor expected. Say only: 'Ladies and gentlemen [pause] – The Queen.'

## After-dinner speaking

Pick a good moment – not when something else may happen. Glance at your notes to remind yourself of your first words. Stand up. Keep still. Look at your audience and nothing else. Imagine them falling silent – they will, but it will seem to take an eternity. As the last voices fade, take a breath, then breathe out, relax, breathe in, say, 'Ladies and gentlemen . . .' and off you go, making the audience laugh or applaud as many times as you are able to. So you will need plenty of well-crafted ideas rather than one setpiece joke. All the best after-dinner speakers draw on their own experiences and interpret life, so that is the place to start in your preparations, which will continue until the speech begins: a good speech, as we all know, connects the speaker with the audience, the occasion, the time and the place.

At dinners there are often two speakers: a serious guest – a minister or dignitary – followed by a professional act. A speech-writer is more likely to help the former, and a normally important person is relegated to the warm-up act – one of the trickiest speech-making situations. The serious speaker should be lighter, wittier, more entertaining than usual and, above all, shorter, while remembering the serious point they wish to air. The real work of the occasion may be done in conversation before, during and after dinner rather than during the speech.

## Tributes

Leaving dos are the setting for some of the best, most memorable – and excruciatingly awful – informal speeches. If the luxury of preparation has been forgone and you feel it is your job to 'say a few words' in such circumstances you can safely stick to this formula:

1. Talk about how everyone feels.
2. Say the nicest thing you can think of about them and their work.
3. Find meaning in their leaving/retirement.
4. Wish them well for the future.

If you are the leaver, you'll want to pay tribute to the colleagues and the organisation you have left behind, and unless you have a public point to make and can afford an irreversible parting of the ways it is best to avoid criticising others or stating controversial opinions.

Politicians' resignation speeches are often memorable: the announcement of Michael Portillo's defeat at the 1997 general election was a sign during election night of the scale of Labour's gains. Opinion was divided between those who enjoyed the greatest symbol of public humiliation and those who recognised the emergence of a different Portillo. Now his words seem dignified and revealing:

> *A truly terrible night for the Conservatives. I would have wished to have been part of rebuilding it inside the House of Commons. I can't now do that. I would like to do whatever I can from the wings to help rebuild a great party which has a great future. One thing alone I will not miss and that's all the questions about the leadership.*[6]

From fiction, Bilbo Baggins's speech to the hobbits at his birthday party in *Lord of the Rings* is a fine example of a farewell tribute and includes rhetorical devices, a simple three-point structure and addresses everyone present:

> *My dear people, my dear Bagginses and Boffins, and my dear Tooks and Brandybucks, and Grubbs, and Chubbs, and Burrowses, and Hornblowers, and Bolgers, Bracegirdles, Goodbodies, Brockhouses and Proudfoots. Also my good Sackville-Bagginses that I welcome back at last to Bag End. Today is my one hundred and eleventh birthday: I am eleventy-one today! I hope you are enjoying yourselves as much as I am. I shall not keep you long. I have called you all together for a Purpose. Indeed for Three Purposes! First of all, to tell you that I am immensely fond of you all, and that eleventy-one years is too short a time to live among such excellent and admirable hobbits. I don't know half of you as well as I should like; and I like less than half of you half as well as you deserve. Secondly to celebrate my birthday. I should say OUR birthday. For it is, of course, also the birthday of my*

*heir and nephew, Frodo. He comes of age and into his inheritance today. Together we score one hundred and forty-four. Your numbers were chosen to fit this remarkable total: One Gross, if I may use the expression. It is also, if I may be allowed to refer to ancient history, the anniversary of my arrival by barrel at Esgaroth on the Long Lake; though the fact that it was my birthday slipped my memory on that occasion. I was only fifty-one then, and birthdays did not seem so important. The banquet was very splendid, however though I had a bad cold at the time, I remember, and could only say 'thag you very buch'. I now repeat it more correctly: Thank you very much for coming to my little party. Thirdly and finally, I wish to make an ANNOUNCE-MENT. I regret to announce that – though, as I said, eleventy-one years is far too short a time to spend among you – this is the END. I am going. I am leaving NOW. GOODBYE!*[7]

## Appeals

When making an appeal – for action or money – the strategy is the same as that used to win votes in a general election or to argue the case for a community project, to raise millions for an Olympic bid or a few pounds at a coffee morning. People will give when they think that their contribution will be well used, when they have something to give, it's easy to give it and there's a benefit to them in giving. You must believe in your cause, and speak about it with passion, sincerity, commitment and confidence.

The 'Magic Formula/Order out of Chaos' structure (see page 33) works well. Decide which of four possible effects you want to have on the audience: to appeal to the majority or the minority, to appeal to those 'for', or to win over those 'against'. It's best to have clear, perhaps extreme, views: it doesn't work to be too even-handed.

## Media interviews

Media interviews are mini-speeches but are disproportionately powerful because of their huge audience. Work out a simple structure that you can remember without notes. The rhetorical devices in chapter 3 (see pages 42-45), especially lists, puzzles, contrasts, repetition and personal statements, are all useful in shaping a resonant phrase or soundbite. Above all, anticipate the interests of the audience – the interviewer and those to whom the result will be broadcast.

A press statement is a little different, usually a two-to-three-minute speech following the pattern of a press release: the main news comes first, followed by any points necessary to back up or explain the statement. Special rules and skills are involved in handling the press, TV and radio and these are outlined and explored in Politico's *How to Handle the Media* by Nicholas Comfort.

## Candidacy speeches

In candidacy speeches the credibility of the speaker is as important as content. You need to appear credible: the audience wants to decide whether you would be a good person to talk from a platform, one-to-one and at a party. No matter how hard a selection panel tries, it's hard to get away from the subjective opinion of 'does the face fit?'. You also need to show that you are part of the 'club': in a political setting you can do this by making positive references to your party and its members, and negative references to the opposition. Do not make negative remarks about individuals of the opposition or another candidate. Beyond that, the selectors will be looking for evidence of the right skills, the right experience, an understanding of what the role involves and what you will do for those you will represent.

## Weddings

Wedding speeches are simply toasts – and you know how to do that (see page 78). They are among the commonest speeches made but also the most anxiety-provoking.

In the 'traditionally English' pattern of speeches, the groom toasts the bridesmaids when you might think he had eyes only for his bride; the bride says nothing, and the responsible role of compère is given to the best man, who is traditionally the most irresponsible person present.

So why bother with speeches? Guests have told me that weddings aren't complete without speeches. And if there are no set speeches the gate is left open for impromptu ones, which can get out of hand. Here are some alternatives:

1. One speech, a toast to the bride and groom.
2. A range of speeches – any combination you like. Have an anchorman or woman to introduce each speaker; make sure they know the running order, what they are talking about, who they are toasting.
3. Go for the traditional – but only if you have the speechmaking resources.

Wedding speeches have jobs to do:
- welcome the guests
- wish the bride and groom well
- remember absent family and guests
- thank parents
- thank hosts
- thank helpers.

Their main point, though, is to tell the story of how the couple got together and will live happily ever after. A wedding marks the end of one relationship with the couple and the beginning of another. The family, the guests and the couple have to make that transition, and the purpose of the speeches is to help them do so. As a speaker you provide a service. Make the audience smile rather than laugh, say, 'Ah' rather than, 'Ouch'. These are feel-good speeches.

The easiest way to prepare a wedding speech is to think of answers to the following questions. You can probably find several answers to the same question, all of them true, but the best one to use will be the one that is most personal to you and best captures the mood of the audience. Jot down the first things that come into your mind.

The introduction and welcome to the guests:
- Welcome. What's really special about this occasion?
- Who is missing? This is a cue for messages from absent family and friends.
- What was the most memorable moment of the day?
- Introduce next speaker.

About the bride:
- Which of her outstanding characteristics can you trace back to her childhood? How?
- What is your favourite memory of her?
- How do you feel at seeing her married?
- What do you wish her in her married life?

Relevant to all:
- What are you enjoying most about the wedding day?
- What's your favourite memory of the bride/groom/parents?
- How did you first meet them and what impression did that make?

- How does he/she make their mark on things?
- What advice/words of wisdom would you give to the person you are toasting?
- Do you have a poem or reading?
- Whom should you thank and what for?
- What do you love about him/her?
- What does it feel like to be married?
- What's the best thing about being (just) married?

A wedding is a time for hyperbole – exaggeration:
- Best parents in the world
- Most beautiful bride
- Handsomest husband
- Happiest marriage
- I will love you for ever
- From here to eternity.

Still stuck? Birth, birthdays, turning-points, childhood, toys, pets, education, friends, home, siblings, family gatherings, holidays, travels, talents, successes, pride and joy, interests, sports, ambitions, vocations are all sources of stories.

Prepare as much as you can remember comfortably without needing a script, but keep a note of names: a wedding is an occasion where getting the names right counts a great deal.

All families have politics and it is best to be aware of them. In sensitive situations decide first if you need to raise them in your speech. Single-parent families, step-parents, second marriages, recent bereavements are the usual problems, and it is best to steer away from any negative reference. If you leave them out altogether, though, they will be so conspicuous by their absence that you will seem to be evading the problem. If you must raise a note of sadness, like a bereavement, do it in the middle of the speech which will leave you plenty of time to move away from the past and end on a positive note about the future.

At least you will know from the guest list exactly who will be there: go through it and make sure there is something in your speech to please everyone. Ask the advice of the couple.

There are few 'don'ts' in speechmaking, but at weddings:

- Don't use sample speeches – you are your own expert
- Don't drink too much
- Don't offend anyone
- Don't go on too long – a couple of minutes is fine.

Please don't include any nasty shocks of the sort that Hugh Grant's character produced in *Four Weddings and a Funeral*:

> *Ladies and gentlemen, this is only the second time I've ever been a best man. I hope I did the job all right last time. The couple in question are at least still talking to me. Unfortunately they're not talking to each other, but I'm sure that has absolutely nothing to do with me. Apparently Paula knew Piers had slept with her younger sister before I mentioned it in my speech. The fact that he had slept with her mother came as a surprise.*[8]

Finally, consider using a visual aid. Your speech is competing in a high-intensity visual experience, with flowers, frocks, cakes, cars and decorations. At a wedding props often work: photographs, gifts, interesting possessions, memorabilia and, where appropriate, a kiss.

## Funerals

The main task for a speaker at a funeral is to put into words what the mourners feel but have been unable to express. Delivering a funeral oration may help your own grieving process too. It should be structured in three parts:

1. The present: purpose of the day, how everyone feels
2. The past: about the person who has died, your own recollections and the audience's
3. The future: a thought for the future, a meaning in the loss.

This was how Tony Blair structured the speech he made the morning after the death of Diana, Princess of Wales (see page 28). Some of the questions most relevant to your speech might be:

- What's the best honest truth about the person who has died?
- What were their best qualities: at work, in public, at leisure, at home, in the family, as a friend?
- What memories from your own experience illustrate those qualities?
- What was it like knowing this person?
- What were their passions?
- What were the highlights of their life?
- What did their family mean to them?
- Who else was close to them?
- How do you say farewell?
- What might comfort the bereaved?
- What is the meaning of their death?

It may help to think of the eulogy as a painting of the person. It needs both a background and a foreground, a general impression and some telling detail, a focus of attention and a frame – all executed in the unique style of the artist. Don't be too solemn or dwell on suffering; don't make factual errors; don't give away secrets.

## Special occasions, interesting questions

A quick method of working out the content of the speech is ask yourself the questions to which you and the audience would like answers. Make a list of as many as you can think of. Then choose the most interesting and make the answers the subject of your speech. The questions below are appropriate to a range of special occasions.

| Occasion | Questions |
|---|---|
| 'Say a few words' | 1.What are you enjoying/feeling about being here? |
| | 2. What is sincere and true for all the audience? |
| | 3. What do you need to do for the audience? |
| | This formula works well for many occasions, including most of those mentioned below. |
| Presenting an award | 1. What is the award for? |
| | 2. Why is the award important? |
| | 3. Why does the winner deserve the award? |
| | 4. How is the audience interested in the winner/award? |
| | 5. How did the winner's personal qualities shine through? |
| | 6. How did the other candidates/entrants fare? |
| | 7. How will the award benefit others? |
| | 8. Who are you making the award to? |
| Accepting an award | 1. Who do you need to thank for the award? |
| | 2. What does the donor mean to you? |
| | 3. Who helped you win and how? |
| | 4. What benefit will the award give you? |
| | 5. What would you say to those following? |
| Introducing a speaker | 1. Why are you pleased to introduce the speaker? |
| | 2. What is important about what the speaker has to say? |
| | 3. What is uniquely interesting about the speaker? |
| | 4. What is the speaker's name, title and role? |

For questions for speeches for weddings and funerals see pages 84-87

| Occasion | Questions |
| --- | --- |
| Vote of thanks | 1. What's the greatest tribute you can make?<br>2. Why have you been honoured to hear X speak?<br>3. What made their speech interesting/fascinating/funny?<br>4. What good wishes can you give to the speaker? |
| Visits | 1. What is the significance of the venue?<br>2. What are you enjoying about being there?<br>3. What can you say that is sincere and true about the staff?<br>4. Why is the occasion important?<br>5. Who do you need to thank and for what?<br>6. What thought can you leave with the audience? |
| Toasts | 1. What makes this gathering special?<br>2. What are we all enjoying about the occasion?<br>3. What's the greatest tribute you can make? |
| Appeals | 1. Why are you speaking?<br>2. What makes this 'a good cause'?<br>3. How much money do you want? |
| Candidacy speeches | 1. What do you feel about the honour of being chosen?<br>2. Do you understand the main requirement of office?<br>3. What's the main skill and experience you bring?<br>4. How will you carry out the office?<br>5. What will you do for those you represent?<br>6. What details support your claim? |

## Debates

When you are preparing for a debate, start by thinking about what the opposition will say. You will know the issues and perhaps the opposition speaker and their position on those issues. Researching the opposing case and speaker will give you a fairly good idea of their attack and defence. You will also discover the points you must address. By the time you have prepared your responses, you will probably have the best part of your speech drafted.

A debate is verbal combat and you need to be in the right mood for it: read some great speeches, a courtroom drama, watch a football match or an episode of *Robot Wars*, in which 'style, control, damage and aggression' are the criteria on which the duels are judged; they apply equally well to a major debate.

Sometimes you will know before you start if you are on the winning side. A government minister is generally on the winning side: the Magic Formula approach or Order out of Chaos works well (see chapter 2, pages 33-35). If you will be on the losing side, your tactics should involve starting with common ground, then challenging the audience to rethink their position, to leave the crowd of the unthinking majority and join the minority élite that stands outside popular opinion. The Agree, But, So structure (see pages 22-23) may be useful. You can make another early decision on tactics from an analysis of the audience's interests: can you safely address them collectively on the assumption that they have a common foe or shared values? Or is your first task to divide the audience and convince one side to accept the view of the other? Do different parts of the audience have different interests? A debate speech must deal with the audience's objections, the information they need to make a favourable decision, and what they should do next.

Never lose sight of the purposes of a debate, which are to stimulate more debate, to win a vote and generally to entertain.

## Conferences and lectures

The keynote speech at a conference is typical of the longer speech that anyone in a senior position is likely to deliver from time to time. No rules are infallible; no formula is universal. You could begin your preparation by looking at the subject from all angles: economic, social, political, moral, scientific/technological/medical, ecological/environmental, legal, international, historical, artistic, psychological, philosophical or, for a government speech, from each aspect of government responsibility. From that you will be able to identify what is most interesting for you and your audience, and be able to set your address within a big picture.

You might like to shape your speech as a story, aiming towards peace, happiness, success, or whatever else you and the audience most value. Perhaps your theme resembles one from a classic, such as virtue recognised (Cinderella), the small person who has the power (*Lord of the Rings*) or smart working (Hercules), in which case you will tell your story within a similar pattern.

A lecture is perhaps two or three times the length of most speeches. If you are a regular speechmaker and are invited to deliver a lecture, regard it as an opportunity to develop a hypothesis that otherwise would not be aired. Speak about something important rather than 'giving a talk'. You will need to open with the hypothesis, so 'one thesis, three points, one conclusion' (see page 31) is the most likely structure. All the evidence of the lecture will support the hypothesis and you will have time to explain in more depth than usual.

Senior people sometimes find themselves having to speak when they have little new to say. They accepted the invitation because it seemed like a good opportunity to make some important announcement, but the announcement has been delayed and they have a long time to fill. One way round this is to go for the history of the subject, which can be expanded to any length, and made interesting; if nothing else, the speech will add to the audience's understanding of the subject.

Educational lectures are not strictly speeches, although lecturers may use speechmaking techniques. Many feel that their task is to include everything they know on the subject, which is a strain for them and, often, dull for their audience. Those who learn to make their lectures more like speeches find it a great relief. It is much easier to be yourself and more interesting for the audience. Whether or not the audience remembers what was said depends partly on how well the lecturer structured their thoughts and language. Lecturers can learn much about how to develop their style from the attention speechmakers give to performance (see also chapter 8, pages 147-154).

## Parliamentary speeches

The work of parliaments and assemblies within any democratic system is performed through speeches. Every parliament has its own conventions: in the UK Parliament, speeches are addressed not to the audience but to one person, the Speaker, who listens to them but doesn't make any; adjournment debates have nothing to do with the adjournment of business; the Official Record may be different from what was actually said.

All MPs make their début in a 'maiden speech' to the House of Commons. This is the first and last occasion when the MP can expect to be called by name (rather than by constituency), not to be interrupted and to receive congratulations. The traditional pattern is to talk glowingly about one's predecessor, about the constituency and to avoid controversy. So, should you stick with tradition or be controversial? Recent history suggests that the latter may be best. Of the three most recent British prime ministers, only John Major respected the House's conventions with a modest speech about local-government grants to his constituency, in the Budget debate of 1979. Characteristically, Margaret Thatcher sidestepped references to both her predecessor and her constituency, in a Private Member's Bill in 1960: 'This is a maiden speech but I know that the constituency of Finchley which I have the honour to represent would not wish me to do other than come straight to the point.' In 1983 Tony Blair broke with tradition and outlined his personal creed:

> *I am a socialist not through reading a textbook that has caught my intellectual fancy, nor through unthinking tradition, but because I believe that, at its best, socialism corresponds most closely to an existence that is both rational and moral. It stands for co-operation, not confrontation; for fellowship not fear. It stands for equality, not because it wants people to be the same but because only through equality in our economic circumstances can our individuality develop properly.*

He used elements of a style to which I referred earlier, the 'negative first', as in, 'I am a socialist not because . . . but . . .', and the 'not only . . . but also' formula, which has been described as 'pervading the political discourse of New Labour in a variety of expressions which both draws attention to assumed incompatibilities, and denies them'.[9]

After their maiden speech, MPs learn parliamentary speech-making through contributing to debates. The craft remains important throughout their parliamentary career. Debate speeches are most effective when they present a convincing case for one side or the other, relate the principle to the lives of individuals, make the particular view the general one, and draw the House's attention to something of which its members may not have been aware. Here is an extract from one of Tony Benn's many speeches on Iraq:

> *War is easy to talk about; there are not many people left of the generation which remembers it. The right hon. member for Old Bexley and Sidcup served with distinction in the last war. I never killed anyone but I wore uniform. I was in London during the blitz in 1940, living where the Millbank tower now stands, where I was born. Some different ideas have come in there since. Every night, I went to the shelter in Thames house. Every morning, I saw docklands burning. Five hundred people were killed in Westminster one night by a land mine. It was terrifying. Are not Arabs and Iraqis terrified? Do not Arab and Iraqi women weep when their children die? Does not bombing strengthen their determination? What fools we are to live as if war is a computer game for our children or just an interesting little Channel 4 news item.*[10]

When MPs become ministers, they have a wider range of speeches to tackle. For the first time they might have the support of a speechwriter.

### Statements

A statement is speechwriting at its most refined and most formal. In relatively few words (below two thousand), it must convince all sides of the House of the need for the proposed action, seek agreement for the strategic intent of the changes, make highly technical proposals easily understood and gain general acceptance for the next stages. In drafting the speech, it helps to rise above the detail and present the bigger picture. Here are some extracts from the statement Tony Blair made on the publication of the dossier on Iraq's weapons of mass destruction, 24 September 2002:

> *At any time, he* [Saddam Hussein] *could have let the inspectors back in and put the world to proof. At any time, he could have co-operated with the United Nations. Ten days ago, he made the offer unconditionally under threat of war. He could have done it at any time in the last eleven years, but he did not. Why?*
>
> *The dossier that we publish gives the answer. The reason is that his chemical, biological and nuclear weapons programme is not an historic left-over from 1998. The inspectors are not needed to clean up the old remains. His weapons-of-mass-destruction programme is active, detailed and growing. The policy of containment is not working. The weapons-of-mass-destruction programme is not shut down: it is up and running now.*
>
> *The dossier is based on the work of the British Joint Intelligence Committee. For over sixty years, beginning just before World War Two, the JIC has provided intelligence assessments to British prime ministers. Normally its work is obviously secret. Unusually, because it is important that we explain our concerns about Saddam to the British people, we have decided to disclose its assessments.*
>
> *I am aware, of course, that people will have to take elements of this on the good faith of our intelligence services, but this is what they are telling me, the British Prime Minister, and my senior colleagues. The intelligence picture that they paint is one accumulated over the last four years. It is extensive, detailed and authoritative. It concludes that Iraq has chemical and biological weapons, that Saddam has continued to produce*

*them, that he has existing and active military plans for the use of chemical and biological weapons, which could be activated within forty-five minutes, including against his own Shia population, and that he is actively trying to acquire nuclear weapons capability.*[11]

'Personal statements' are often resignation speeches and interesting for what they reveal about the parting of the ways, criticism of the leadership, implied or explicit, and the speaker's view of what might have been. Robin Cook's resignation speech, delivered six months after the above, starts with a personal statement and a light touch, immediately linking him to the majority of the audience: 'This is the first time for twenty years that I have addressed the House from the back benches. I must confess that I had forgotten how much better the view is from here.'

He goes on to contradict Tony Blair's statement with a mixture of facts, contrasts and rhetorical questions:

*For four years as Foreign Secretary I was partly responsible for the western strategy of containment. Over the past decade that strategy destroyed more weapons than in the Gulf War, dismantled Iraq's nuclear-weapons programme and halted Saddam's medium- and long-range missiles programmes. Iraq's military strength is now less than half its size than at the time of the last Gulf War.*

*Ironically, it is only because Iraq's military forces are so weak that we can even contemplate its invasion. Some advocates of conflict claim that Saddam's forces are so weak, so demoralised and so badly equipped that the war will be over in a few days. We cannot base our military strategy on the assumption that Saddam is weak and at the same time justify pre-emptive action on the claim that he is a threat.*

*Iraq probably has no weapons of mass destruction in the commonly understood sense of the term – namely, a credible device capable of being delivered against a strategic city target. It probably still has biological toxins and battlefield chemical munitions, but it has had them since the 1980s when US companies sold Saddam anthrax agents and the then British government approved chemical and munitions factories. Why is it now so urgent that we should take military action to disarm a military capacity that has been there for twenty years, and which we helped to create? Why is it necessary to resort to war this week, while Saddam's ambition to complete his weapons programme is blocked by the presence of UN inspectors?*

*What has come to trouble me most over past weeks is the suspicion that if the hanging chads in Florida had gone the other way and Al Gore had been elected, we would not now be about to commit British troops.*

*The longer that I have served in this place, the greater the respect I have for the good sense and collective wisdom of the British people. On Iraq, I believe that the prevailing mood of the British people is sound. They do not doubt that Saddam is a brutal dictator, but they are not persuaded that he is a clear and present danger to Britain.*[12]

## Speeches for legislation

Legislation requires a whole suite of speeches. The second reading debate is the first and main opportunity to debate the proposals. Its two main speeches require very different handling:

**Opening speech** The main purpose is to generate a good debate. It is a showcase for the legislation, so is generally given by a senior minister, often the secretary of state. It presents evidence for the supporting arguments. Keep in sight the effect of the proposed legislation on individuals and reserve some points for responses to likely interventions. Hence the importance of thorough research and preparation. The speech should be long enough to start the debate, but not so long that it shortens it – about twenty minutes maximum, plus ten minutes for interventions.

**Closing speech** The purpose is to repeat the main strands of the Government's case, on a positive note, while responding to points raised during the debate. Much of the hard work is done during the debate by the minister, who has to assimilate the debate and synthesise a response. A speechwriter can support them by providing an outline of the key points to make and being ready with speaking notes for likely topics.

### Adjournment debates

Adjournment debates were named from the debates that took place when a sitting ends. They are short – generally thirty to ninety minutes – and on subjects that would otherwise not find a slot in the main parliamentary programme. They provide opportunities for:

- A backbencher to raise a debate on a subject of his or her choice and to receive a reply from a minister.
- Government to initiate debate without there being a motion for resolution. It is a device to avoid a division on a matter of substance; for example the report of the Royal Commission on Long-term Care for the Elderly.

- Emergency debates: they occur rarely – about once per parliamentary session. A backbencher gives a three-minute speech on an important subject leading to a three-hour debate.

Most of the debates that take place in the second debating chamber, Westminster Hall, are adjournment debates. When a backbencher opens an adjournment debate, their speech should spark general interest, while being obscure and specific enough to make the minister work hard in their response. Ideally, it should demand an outcome that the minister can satisfy.

If you are preparing the minister's speech, you will need:

- to research; fortunately, it is usual to consult the backbencher so that you have some idea what to expect
- a full draft of the opening and closing paragraphs
- a clear draft of any announcements – adjournment debates are increasingly being used by ministers to make announcements for which parliamentary time would otherwise not be available
- a longer draft than you think will be needed, with optional sections marked. The minister speaks at the end of the debate, so he or she will not know how long his speech should be or exactly what it should contain.

## Opposition days and other special debates

A number of days are allocated during the parliamentary year for the opposition to call a whole-day debate. The topics are inevitably controversial, and the warning given may be only a few days, with the opposition objective revealed on the day before when they put down their motion. The speechwriter will need all the resources and judgement available to them to assemble material for the minister (generally a secretary of state) to reply to the opposition's opening speech with an opposing motion.

These are often the best debates, and for four years, from 1993 to 1997, Kenneth Clarke and Gordon Brown, as chancellor and shadow chancellor respectively, regularly entertained the House to heavyweight oratory. Here is a short sample from an hour of combat during the last of six days' debate on the Queen's Speech in October 1996.[13] The debate was on an opposition amendment when Brown baited the chancellor about the rise in interest rates:

> *I tell the Chancellor of the Exchequer: prudence is absolutely critical to the economy, which is why the interest rate rise was necessary – the one that he has been forced to make – but prudent economic management depends for its success on the firm foundation of a strong economy that is investment rich, and he has failed to achieve. Without investment-led growth and the export-led and industry-led recovery that was promised, we get to the problems that the Chancellor faces today.*

Clarke responded:

> *The right hon. gentleman must watch me taking decisions with which he reluctantly agrees and which are keeping us on course. I have achieved such a low-inflation climate that I am able to move interest rates by small amounts. I am sure that no hon. member can remember when we last saw an increase in interest rates of only a quarter of one per cent. Past chancellors would have given their eye teeth to live in a world where they moved interest rates by only twenty-five basis points, or a quarter of one per cent. We can all remember rates going up by one per cent, half a percent or even two per cent.*

## Parliamentary protocols

All parliaments and assemblies have their own protocols for speeches. In the House of Commons, for instance, 'The Right Honourable Gentleman' or 'Lady' is used to refer to members of the Privy Council, 'My Honourable Friend' refers to a member of the same side, while 'The Honourable Member' refers to an opposition MP. Some MPs still use 'the Honourable and Learned' when mentioning an MP who is also a QC, although the protocol was discontinued following the 1997 modernisation of proceedings. If you write or give parliamentary speeches, you will need to know exactly what the conventions are. Various sources of advice are available, from publications such as Dod's Parliamentary Companion to specialists in the House; all government departments have a Parliamentary Unit to advise their staff.

What is said in parliaments is always recorded in an Official Record, which in the UK is Hansard. It helps if speakers can provide a copy of their speech, ideally electronically, with proof of the source of any quotations used so that details can be verified for the published version.

Finally, if you are helping a parliamentary speaker, you may have to provide handwritten speaking notes in response to points raised during the debate. Civil servants refer to them as 'box notes' because they are prepared in 'The Box', a wooden pen between the front bench and the Speaker's chair where a small team sits during important ministerial debates. Try to draft box notes with style, so that they are presentationally effective, but at the very least write legibly!

## Go on, make a speech

Every speech is unique: what you say has never been said before, and the occasion has never happened before. That is why there are no sample speeches in this book. The most important ingredient in a speech is the way it links the speaker, the audience, the subject, the occasion, the time and the place. No sample speech can do that.

Of course, on some occasions there are too many speeches: the record must be the World Summit in Johannesburg in 2002 where seventy world leaders each gave a five-minute speech in an eleven-hour day of rhetoric. But without a speech, most special occasions can fall a little flat.

I enjoy writing for small occasions, and I encourage speechwriters to grab these speeches when they see them coming up. If someone gives a lot of important speeches, they will probably make minor ones too. They won't have much time to prepare, and their staff may think the occasion is too far down the scale of importance to brief a speechwriter to prepare anything. But a relaxed, intimate and more private gathering is the place to air material that would be unsuitable in a public arena. In such circumstances the speaker can experiment with new techniques, test-run passages of the speech or a style of delivery for a bigger occasion. They can have fun and so will the audience.

# Five

# Hearts and minds

A great speech bears the imprint of the speaker's mind and heart, their character and soul. In this chapter we will look at how to tailor a speech to a perfect fit for the speaker, using traditional skills and psychology.

A speech will affect each member of the audience differently. Some may be enthused, some interested, others bored, and a few indifferent. There has to be something in the speech for everyone. Psychology offers several tools that will help you achieve this.

## Head, heart and guts: the influencing-styles triangle

From persuading a nation to support war to asking guests to join in a toast, every speech is an act of influence, of which there are three styles. We all tend to prefer one style above the others.

- The **tough battler** hammers home their point, perhaps by repeating it forcefully. Their influencing is accompanied by imperatives – shoulds, musts, oughts – and their speech is delivered uncompromisingly, perhaps accompanied by physical gestures such as banging a fist.
- The **logical thinker** appeals to reason, with an argument that is rational, factual, logical, cool, unemotional and authoritative.

- The **friendly helper** identifies with the listener by establishing a common purpose, interest or understanding. They make friends to influence people.

In a crisis, the Tough Battler will tell everyone what to do and offer no alternatives; the Logical Thinker explains the situation and the rationality of a course of action; the Friendly Helper befriends the listeners.

The influencing style of a speaker seems to be one of the dominant characteristics of the way they present themselves; it is generally easy to identify and hard to mask.

### The influencing-skills triangle

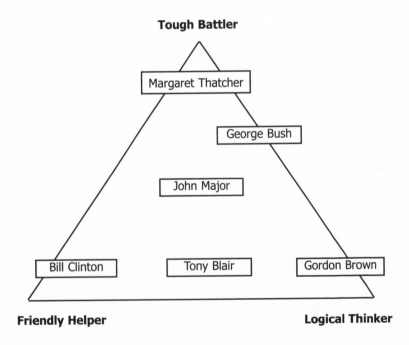

When I suggest this model to students, there is general agreement about recent British prime ministers and American presidents. Margaret Thatcher is a 'Tough Battler', as is George Bush. Bill Clinton is a 'Friendly Helper', a style he has consistently maintained, even in his lengthy autobiography, which reads like an epic fireside chat. Fashions change: since the mid-1990s the Friendly Helper corner has been the one to go for. Tony Blair is a lawyer by training and his early speeches would have left most people in no doubt that he was a 'Logical Thinker'. Here is an extract from a lecture he gave in Perth, Australia, a forensic analysis of the state of the Labour Party in 1982, the year before he entered Parliament, with a hint of his future strategy to unite the party:

> First, the party appeal must encompass more than the traditional working-class elements of the electorate. To put it crudely, an appeal that reaches only the NUM and the Guardian letter-writers is not going to win Labour a general election. This is straightforward, obvious, psychological sense. But it is remarkable how often it is ignored. The Left is fond of pointing to the radicalism of early socialists as justification for their own views. If that means the Left should draw on the spirit of party founders, that is positive; if it means a blind obedience to traditional doctrine, that is misguided ativism.[1]

However, he has since become more of a 'Friendly Helper': he has the capacity to make an audience feel that they are the only people in the world who matter to him. But a change of style can bring with it the risk of not sounding natural and sincere. The Logical Thinker stance, as represented by Gordon Brown, is unfashionable. As prime minister, John Major didn't seem to conform strongly to any of the three styles, but he was one of the most tough, determined politicians I have encountered.

Speechwriters know that all three styles must come through in a good speech. In the film *Braveheart*, William Wallace's speech to the Scottish army at the battle of Stirling is scripted to show them:

> *Sons of Scotland, I am William Wallace, and I see a whole army of my countrymen here in defiance of tyranny. You have come to fight as free men, and free men you are. What will you do with that freedom? Will you fight? Fight and you may die. Run and you will live, at least for a while. And dying in your beds, many years from now, would you be willing to trade all the days from this day to that for one chance, just one chance, to come back and tell our enemies they may take our lives, but they will never take our freedom. Scotland the Brave.*[2]

It starts with the identification of self and the audience, the Friendly Helper, moves on to the arguments for fighting or fleeing through a series of questions and contrasts, the Logical Thinker, and ends with an uncompromising rallying call, the Tough Battler. It was based on reports of the actual thirteenth-century speech.

An expert speaker adopts all three styles and moves between them during a speech. They start in their natural style, develop their arguments through their second preference, perhaps including the one with which they feel least comfortable, and finish in the style with which they began. Inexperienced speakers tend to stick to the one style they prefer and their speeches may sound incomplete.

For the speechwriter, the challenge is to identify the speaker's style and write to it. You can help a speaker with good writing in their least preferred style. Try to understand your own style: if you are a Friendly Helper, you may have to put aside your own style to write for a Tough Battler, you can complement the speaker's style with your own input.

All of the above can be simplified even further. The influencing-skills triangle equates to the everyday notion of 'head' (Logical Thinker), 'heart' (Friendly Helper) and 'guts' (Tough Battler). An effective speech needs all three. Add 'head' with confident, interesting facts and examples, rationality and reason. Include 'heart' with warmth and friendliness, or with drama, shock and emotion. For 'guts', go straight to the point forcefully.

Bill Clinton's televised address after he had testified to the Grand Jury about his relationship with Monica Lewinsky drew on all his skills to bring the American people back to his side. In the following extract, observe how he used different styles for different purposes, and the balance between them:

> *Good evening. This afternoon in this room, from this chair, I testified before the Office of Independent Counsel and the grand jury.*[3]

Deprived of the opportunity to be his usual friendly self – the audience was in no mood for warmth – he began in the simplest way possible. He went on to state the situation with incontrovertible facts. This was a counterweight to the doubts that were to come and the start of a negotiation with the audience:

> *I answered their questions truthfully, including questions about my private life, questions no American citizen would ever want to answer.*

With this he established that he had the same feelings as his audience, which linked into his confession, the 'heart' of the speech:

> *Indeed I did have a relationship with Ms Lewinsky that was*
> *not appropriate. In fact it was wrong. I misled people,*
> *including even my own wife. I deeply regret that.*

'It was wrong' and 'I deeply regret that' are the shortest sentences of
the speech and so have the greatest emphasis. They make his pecca-
dillo sound more shocking than if he had misled the courts or the
public. At this point the speech changed tack into the reasons for the
deception: the 'head' part. As Clinton moved away from his preferred
style, the crafting became clumsy. One sentence is forty-seven words
long – hard to read without stumbling and difficult to follow:

> *In addition, I had real and serious concerns about an inde-*
> *pendent counsel investigation that began with private business*
> *dealings twenty years ago, dealings, I might add, about which*
> *an independent federal agency found no evidence of any wrong-*
> *doing by me or my wife over two years ago.*

Time to add some 'guts' and get tough, for which he used repetition
and imperatives:

> *And now the investigation itself is under investigation. This has*
> *gone on too long, cost too much, and hurt too many innocent*
> *people. Now this matter is between me, the two people I love*
> *most – my wife and our daughter – and our God. I must put it*
> *right . . . Nothing is more important to me personally. But it is*
> *private, and I intend to reclaim my family life for my family.*
> *It's nobody's business but ours.*

Then he deflected from the private and present by switching to
national concerns and the future:

> *It is time to stop the pursuit of personal destruction and the*
> *prying eyes and get on with national life.*

A few sentences later there was an extraordinary twist: he implied that, in following the scandal, the American people might have forgotten about national issues and compromised security:

> *We have important work to do – real opportunities to seize, real*
> *problems to solve, real security matters to face. And so tonight, I*
> *ask you to turn away from the spectacle of the past seven months,*
> *to repair the fabric of our national discourse, and to return our*
> *attention to all the challenges and all the promise of the next*
> *American century. Thank you for watching. And good night.*

If in doubt, a safe formula for most speeches is to follow the one Bill Clinton adopted:

1. Heart: start by making friendly connections with and showing understanding of the audience
2. Head: present the main subject in a rational way
3. Guts: add a little toughness, if necessary
4. Heart: close with a warm, uplifting conclusion.

Improving the balance of these three elements is one of the easiest and most dramatic ways of improving a speech.

## Aristotle's three appeals: ethos, pathos, logos

Two thousand years ago, Aristotle identified the influencing forces in a speech and described how persuasion works by registering three 'appeals' with the audience:

- **Ethos** proves the speaker's credibility. It is the appeal of the speaker for who they are.
- **Pathos** is the emotional appeal of the speech. It is about feelings, from passionate to considerate. Pathos wins hearts, knowing that minds will follow.
- **Logos** is the appeal to reason. It makes the logical, rational case for the speech. Logos is being right.

The 'three appeals' informs the speaker of the best way to connect with an audience. It applies to all aspects of a speech.

Establish *ethos* by:

- telling the audience who you are and your role
- drawing on personal authoritative experience
- adopting a positive attitude
- stressing nouns rather than adjectives or verbs
- dressing and using body language appropriate to the occasion.

Without ethos, the audience is unlikely to believe or trust a speaker, however logical or passionate their case. Ethos will be lacking if the speaker:

- fails to tell the audience who they are or why they are there; hence the importance of introductions
- gives insufficient evidence that they know what they are talking about
- is apologetic, conditional, unprepared, flustered, negative
- their dress and body language conflict with the task of the speech.

Establish *pathos* by:

- reflecting common likes and values
- accurately assessing the mood of the occasion and the audience
- revealing something of your own emotions
- talking with feeling about the issues of 'logos' and 'pathos', adding an image often works, presenting the case as stories
- stressing adjectives rather than verbs or nouns
- identifying the issues with the strongest emotional appeal for the occasion.

Without pathos, an audience will probably not like what they hear, whoever the speaker is and however logical their case. Pathos will be lacking if the speaker:

- distances themselves from the audience
- fails to sum up the mood of the occasion and the audience
- hides or misrepresents their own emotions
- overlooks the issues the audience feels most strongly about.

Establish *logos* by:

- providing evidence, examples, facts to support the case
- marshalling information that the audience knows
- stressing verbs rather than nouns or adjectives
- presenting new evidence.

Without logos, an audience is unlikely to conclude that they agree with what they hear, whoever the speaker is and however passionately they feel about the subject. Logos will be lacking if:

- assumptions are presented without proof
- the evidence is weak
- the evidence is incomplete.

## The four elements

Another ancient model draws on the images of earth, air, water and fire. In a good speech the four are balanced:

1. add more earth with illustrations, facts and figures, examples, experience, demonstrations of how things work
2. add more air with ideas, visions, change, possibilities
3. add more water with emotion, personal views, values, empathy and understanding
4. add more fire with purpose, energy, action, passion and commitment.

If a speech draft sounds flat, adjust the balance of the elements to make it come alive.

## Learners and teachers

Some speeches and all lectures involve the audience in learning something new, which can be a satisfying experience. Learning takes place as a circle that students enter at different places, according to their own preferred style of learning, then travel round. The four styles, each relating to an element, are known as Activists (fire), Reflectors (water), Theorists (air) and Pragmatists (earth)[4] and are easy to define with a practical example, such as using a new video-recorder. The Activist plugs in the machine, loads in a tape and presses the buttons that worked the old machine to see what happens. The

Reflector starts by noting some of the differences between the old machine and the new one. The Theorist finds out everything that the new model is designed to do. The Pragmatist reads the instruction book. To learn how to use the new video-recorder involves four stages, not one, or the Theorist will know what the new machine can do but not get it to work, while the Activist will get it to work but understand only a fraction of what it can do, and so on.

Problems occur when the four styles are unbalanced. Tony Blair's style is naturally 'Theorist'. I once counted fifty-three assertions of theory unrelated to practice in one of his speeches: it sounded short on substance and, at worst, as though he was talking to himself.

## Leaders and followers

As well as being an act of persuasion, a speech is invariably an act of leadership. Leaders have obvious characteristics of authority, vision and the means to achieve that vision. Recent research at the London Business School shows that all inspirational leaders also share four unexpected qualities:[5]

1. They reveal weaknesses, which demonstrates approachability and humanity.
2. They rely on intuition, instinctively using a wide range of soft data to gauge when and how to act.
3. They empathise passionately but realistically with those they lead.
4. They reveal their differences, capitalising on what is unique about themselves.

All can be identified in the extracts of Bill Clinton's speeches I have included in this book. A high degree of empathy with the audience is a major component – just old-fashioned charm, really, but more revealing and intuitive in its expression. Diana, Princess of Wales, another great empathiser, was a shy orator but the lasting impression from her best-remembered speech, in which she announced her withdrawal from public life, in December 1993, was her admission of the overwhelming pressures of media exposure and her plea for 'time and space'. She decided the timing of her speech intuitively too, she took her hosts, and the world, by surprise at a routine lunch held by Headway National Head Injuries Association.

Most people would hesitate to use these leadership qualities, or would even employ their opposites: for example, they might conform to a group rather than revealing what sets them apart from it as a credible leader. If they are made aware of these qualities, potential leaders can gain a greater understanding of their own powers, how to develop them, and how to bring them out authentically in their speeches.

People follow those who produce within them three emotional responses:[6]

1. a feeling of significance
2. a feeling of community
3. a feeling of excitement.

These affirmations are better achieved in a speech than by almost any other means.

Did Lieutenant Colonel Tim Collins, speaking to British troops on the eve of war in Iraq, offer leadership?[7] His speech certainly held significance, a sense of community and excitement, with authority, vision and the means to achieve it. His empathy was realistically human – some said it was more realistic than necessary: military leaders of the two world wars didn't remind their soldiers that they might die. He said little about his authority – the 'ethos' (see page 110) – but his status, as a senior figure in the British army, was known to the audience. Here are some reported extracts from the speech:

> *We go to liberate, not to conquer. We will not fly our flags in their country. We are entering Iraq to free a people and the only flag which will be flown on this ancient land is their own. Show respect for them.*
>
> *There are some who are alive at this moment who will not be alive shortly. Those who do not wish to go on that journey, we will not send. As for the others, I expect you to rock their world. Wipe them out if that is what they choose. But if you are ferocious in battle remember to be magnanimous in victory. Iraq is steeped in history. It is the site of the Garden of Eden, the Great Flood and the birthplace of Abraham. Tread lightly there. You will see things that no man could pay to see and you will have to go a long way to find a more decent, generous and upright people than the Iraqis. You will be embarrassed by their hospitality even though they have nothing.*
>
> *Don't treat them as refugees, for they are in their own country. Their children will be poor, in years to come they will know the light of liberation in their lives was brought by you. If there are casualties of war then remember that when they woke up and got dressed in the morning they did not plan to die this day. Allow them dignity in death. Bury them properly and mark their graves.*
>
> *If someone surrenders, ensure that one day they go home to their family. The ones who wish to fight, well, we aim to please. It is my foremost intention to bring every single one of you out alive. But there may be people among us who will not see the*

*end of this campaign. We will put them in their sleeping bags and send them back. There will be no time for sorrow.*

*If you harm your regiment or its history by over-enthusiasm in killing or in cowardice, know it is your family who will suffer. You will be shunned unless your conduct is of the highest order – for your deeds will follow you through history. We will bring shame on neither our uniform nor our nation.*

*The enemy should be in no doubt that we are his nemesis and that we are bringing about his rightful destruction. There are many regional commanders who have stains on their souls and they are stoking the fires of hell for Saddam. He and his forces will be destroyed by this coalition for what they have done. As they die they will know their deeds have brought them to this place. Show them no pity.*

*As for ourselves, let's bring everyone home and leave Iraq a better place for us having been there. Our business now is north.*

## Does gender matter?

Finally, like it or not, it is wise in communication to take account of gender differences. We know quite a bit about how the genders communicate within themselves.[8] Women talking to women tend to establish rapport and find points of connection, strengthening links between them. Men talking to men tend to establish status, and exchange information. In conversation, women ask more questions, make greater use of the pronouns 'you' and 'we'. They use more intensifiers – 'so busy' – more emotive adjectives and emotional exclamations (often empathetic). Men are more likely to introduce new topics to the conversation and to make more declarations of fact or opinion. Writing for an audience of your own sex is relatively easy – just do what comes naturally.

We know little about how communication works across genders. Writing for audiences of the opposite sex can be difficult. My own enquiries suggest that if you are a man speaking to an audience of women, they will appreciate being addressed as if they are of a similar status. If you are a woman speaking to an audience of men, the audience will want you to come straight to the point.

## Heard as human

How well are speakers doing in the quest to appear human? Tim Collins' eve-of-Iraq-war speech (see pages 115-116) scores highly, but other people's efforts often meet with divided opinion. Some were favourably impressed with Michael Howard's 'British Dream' speech of 2004.[9] Others thought it a nightmare:

> *After I left university I spent a year in America. I admire many aspects of American life. In America, they talk about the American Dream. They talk about the ability of someone born in a log cabin to make it to the White House. As it happens, in America this is the exception, not the rule. In Britain it actually does happen. There are countless examples of people from humble beginnings who make it to the top: who live the British Dream. So we should talk about it. We should embrace it. We should celebrate it. I want everyone to live the British Dream. My family and I owe a huge debt to this country. I owe this country everything I have and everything I am. I have now been given a great responsibility by my party. I shall do my utmost to discharge it to the very best of my ability. That means convincing the British people that there is a better way.*

If you were Michael Howard's speechwriter, would you tamper with it? I'd be wary: I like the glimpse of personal experience post-university; I like 'I owe this country everything I have and everything I am', with its echo of a marriage vow. The balance of head, heart and guts seems about right. And it sounds like Michael Howard – 'I admire many aspects of American life' isn't how most other people would say the same thing. He's very good at sounding as if he is saying, 'Well, fancy that' ('I know what causes crime – criminals!'). But I'd want to eliminate two phrases: 'the British people' should be banned from political utterance because of its us-and-them effect; and 'the British Dream', which is too sweeping. Was it an embarrassing nightmare or fair play? We'll find out at the next general election.

I'm always cautious when the topic of conversation turns to the question of who is today's greatest orator. Bill Clinton always emerges near the top of the list – and when he does someone disagrees: they find his warmth insincere. Tony Blair is rated highly at smaller gatherings, but his big conference and setpiece speeches disappoint. In British politics, it is the chancellors and shadow chancellors rather than the prime ministers and party leaders, who, during the last ten years, have been the most consistently powerful speakers: Gordon Brown, Kenneth Clarke, Peter Lilley, Michael Portillo and, more recently, Michael Howard and Oliver Letwin. They all had command of their subject, a memory packed with evidence and argument, which they applied at the right moments. It's hard and perhaps a little unfair to judge the speaker rather than his or her speech. Even William Hague's widely acknowledged skills as a talented speechmaker didn't do him much good at the ballot box.

All writers develop an instinctive feel for the effects of the words they write. They can think round corners, anticipate what the audience needs to hear: is it a question to be answered, a feeling to acknowledge, a new idea to add to the argument, thinking or feeling? They have an eye on where they are leading and an ear for the dull, which is cut from the draft. They can also spot those points in a speech where the audience and the speaker are about to part company: the audience is stuck, struggling to take in some facts, and the speaker is heading off with a new theory. A speech is like a zip, keeping audience and speaker together at every notch.

The theories and models in this chapter are 'ready reckoners'. All are neater as concepts than as descriptions of the way people think and speak. But they are simple to grasp and apply. All can be identified from observation or from readily available information. None require psychometric tests or questionnaires. Even without explicit discussion, as a speechwriter you can gain a quick, unintrusive insight into how your client's mind works. The models will also help you to identify blind spots. In stressful situations, such as giving a speech, we tend to stick to our preferred style rather than widening our range of communication techniques to get the point across. They will help a speechwriter to write as their speaker thinks, thus enabling them to become more successful. With these techniques you can take on the most difficult persuasive tasks with style and success. The best praise a speaker can attract is not to be told that they are a great speaker, or that they have given a great speech, or even that the audience agrees with them, but that the audience has responded positively to what they heard.

As speakers, we are expert in how our own mind works and we may use that knowledge to hone our approach. Great speakers are not made by pretending to be someone else or copying models. 'Be yourself more with skill'[10] is the management advice. The late Bob Monkhouse, a fine after-dinner speaker, put it a little differently: 'Be yourself, made large.'[11]

# Six

# Research

If you have a speechwriter, an assistant who thinks of everything and a wonderful mind that fountains brilliant ideas while you are walking the dog, sitting on a train or fiddling with paperclips, you can safely skip this chapter. If you can think on your feet and have an instinctive feel for your audience then you too can skip it. But most of us, most of the time, need to prepare carefully before we make a speech. Even the smallest speech benefits from prior research, and research for a major speech may take over 90 per cent of the available preparation time. Research provides the answers to two vital questions: What matters? What's interesting? Most of this book has been about answering those questions through the structures that work for different occasions, ways with words for audiences, and the general principles involved in winning hearts and minds. But there are still some gaps to plug.

Too little research is risky, too much wastes time. Research ends only when the speaker begins.

## Research the occasion

The checklist of questions that follows on pages 124–125 covers the essentials for a major speech. The answers will inform both the content of the speech and the logistics of the event. In some ways, preparation for a smaller occasion is harder because a speaker may have to be more self-sufficient. The best preparation is thinking – which is free and can be done anywhere – as Christopher Jary at the Centre for Management and Policy Studies encouragingly reminds speechwriting students. The next best preparation is to establish good contact with the organisers of the event – but remember that their role may be limited to conference organising: you will need to find out through them who really knows what the occasion is about. As early in the preparations as possible, contact the most senior person in the host organisation and ask, 'What would you like me to speak about?' The response you get will inform much of your subsequent preparations. Whether you speak about what you were asked to speak about may be a matter of judgement!

I believe, with most speakers and all audiences, that it is vitally important that what you say is relevant to your audience. When the 2001 general election was announced at a London secondary school, Tony Blair sounded as if he had no particular audience in mind, certainly not the pupils present: 'Mortgage rates half of what they were in the eighties and nineties' and 'Most people, quite rightly, do not pass their time immersed in politics. They have bills to pay, the job to do, the family to raise, the thousand different pressures of everyday life with which to contend.'[1] It wouldn't have taken much tweaking to make the draft relevant, but the task was overlooked.

When you take the trouble to be relevant, an audience will want to listen to you, rather than feeling they ought to. Children make great audiences: they love stories and rehearsing the emotions that go with them. They are thoughtful when they relate experiences to the bigger picture. They like 'head, heart and guts' in giant doses. Professor Susan Greenfield is able to communicate her enthusiasm for brain research way beyond her professional peers. To an audience of children she said:

> When I was first at Oxford and I had to dissect a human brain, let me tell you what it was like. They brought in a kind of Tupperware pot and you had to wear special gloves because the brain was immersed in something to keep it reasonably solid – an evil-smelling and fairly toxic substance. So you wear special gloves, you roll up your sleeves and you prise off the lid and you put your hand in and hold in one hand the essence of a person. Now all of us, increasingly, will be having heart transplants and lung transplants and everything below your eyebrows will be exchanged with someone else's. But would you want a brain transplant? The brain is the essence of you. And I wondered as I held this brain in my hand, 'Say I got a bit under my fingernail . . .' (When I said that once, someone was actually sick I have to say, and we had to stop the lecture quickly.) 'Say I got a bit under my fingernail, would that be the bit that somebody loved with? Or would it be a memory? Or would it be a habit?' All these things that you take for granted, your memories, your habits, your thoughts and your feelings, somehow we have to explain how they are all generated by something, some sludgy little thing that you could get under your fingernail. So that's why I got hooked on doing brain research, because for me this was the most exciting question we could ask.[2]

In the House of Lords, she found a link with her older audience:

> We personalise our brains; we develop a mind. It is this learning, this ability to see one thing in terms of another,

*that I regard as understanding. Far from being some airy-fairy alternative to the squalor of the physical brain, I see the mind as the personalisation of the brain. It is these person-alised connections, sadly, which can be dismantled by conditions such as Alzheimer's disease. As your lordships may know, in such degenerative conditions the patient will gradually recapitulate childhood; gradually the world will mean less and less and gradually the patient will retreat back into the booming and buzzing confusion, where even people and objects that were very dear and close to the patient are no longer recognised. The point I am trying to make is that the competence of our brains, of our mental abilities, rests on the integrity and the extent and number of our brain connec-tions. It is these connections which, in turn, are dependent on the experiences we have in the world.[3]*

It's vital, too, to check and double check the accuracy of what you say about your audience and the occasion, as Whitney Houston discovered when she said a few words at the beginning of a concert in Lisbon, Portugal. She yelled at the audience, 'I love you, Spain.'[4]

## Researching the occasion: a checklist

### 1. The invitation

Is a speech the best medium for the content?

Is the speaker the right speaker?

Is it the best use of the speaker's time?

Should the speech be delivered at all?

Is the person invited first choice?

What would be the total time commitment?

### 2. The occasion

What is it about?

What is the organisation?

What is their business/reputation?

What do they want the speaker to say?

What is the level of formality/informality?

What happened at the same occasion last year?

What significance has the date/year?

What happened on the same day last year, ten years ago, fifty years ago, 100 years ago?

What significance has the occasion?

What is the local context?

### 3. The audience

How big is the audience?

Who are they?

What do they want to hear?

What do they need to hear?

What are their interests/concerns?

What is their frame of reference?

What would make them really happy?

Are there sensitive issues?

Has the speaker addressed the audience previously?

Is there anything the speaker should avoid saying?

Is there anyone the speaker knows/would like to meet/would not like to meet? Where will they be before/during/after the speech?

Will the press be present?

Who should be thanked?

Who should be complimented?

### 4. The speech

What is the purpose of the speech?

Is there a task involved, such as a launch?

How long is the speech?

Does the speaker make/accept an award? If so, to/from whom?

How will the organiser handle interruptions?

Will there be questions and answers?

Is there a panel?

Who is chairing the panel?

Is a printed draft required?

Is a visual presentation necessary/desirable?

## 5. Other speakers

Who else is speaking?

Who is speaking before/after the speaker?

What will they say?

Who, if anyone, is introducing whom?

## 6. The venue

What is the venue?

What significance has the venue?

What are the facilities?

Where will the speaker stand?

Is there a backdrop?

What is the lighting?

How close are the audience?

Is there a lectern or podium?

Is there an autocue?

Is there a microphone? What sort?

What other technology is involved?

Is there a rehearsal?

Can distractions be eliminated?

Can we visit the venue in advance?

## 7. Arrangements with the organiser

Who is the host?

Who is the administrator?

Who is the technician?

Who else will the speaker meet?

How long is the speaker expected to stay?

Is there a reception/lunch/dinner?

Is there a dress code?

Is the speaker required to do anything other than make a speech?

What would be the consequences of late running?

What is the fee (if any)?*

What are the expenses (if any)?*

What are the arrangements for travel, accommodation?*

What are the arrangements for security?*

Who will meet the speaker on arrival?*

*Agree in writing.

## 8. On the day

Do recent events overnight/on the day have a bearing on the speech?

## Researching the subject

When you have made your preparations for a speech you will have plenty of ideas for what to include to make it interesting and entertaining. See also the checklist below for more.

Senior speakers often complain that they have to give the same speech again and again, but no one complains that Pavarotti always sings 'Nessun Dorma'. A trademark speech can be adapted to different audiences. No two speeches are exactly alike because circumstances are different. The foreign secretary, for example, currently speaks frequently about Iraq: last week he may have spoken to diplomats at home; next week he may address soldiers in Iraq. Since last week the situation has moved on, the climate has changed. All speeches should be topical and reflect current mood, so there is always something new to say.

---

**CHECKLIST OF TOPICS TO INCLUDE IN A SPEECH**

---

Who the speaker is and why they are there

Compliments

Thanks – for the invitation, to the audience, the organisers

The unique significance of the date/year

The unique significance of the occasion

The unique significance of the place

Views, vision

Personal experience

All points of agreement/difference with other authorities on the subject

Crisp and complete arguments for/against

Up-to-date, interesting facts and figures, including costs

Case histories involving ordinary people

Connections with people/events in fact and fiction

References in literature

Expand on a definition

Evidence from the wider context, e.g. from different countries

The historical context, then-and-now comparisons

Company/government policy on the subject

Important reports on the subject

Simple, lucid accounts of technical sections

Analogies

Stories that illustrate any of the above

Ideas for wit and humour

The opposition's strengths/weaknesses, attack/defence

Announcements

A new phrase for a soundbite

Good news

Today's news:

- For an entertaining introduction
- For serious comment

Recycled material from other speeches

Proverbs, quotes and clichés to rework

A moral, thought or challenge to take away

## Risk assessment

Now, making a speech is important, and there is an element of risk. To keep the time spent on preparations in proportion to the importance of the occasion, it's useful to do a simple risk assessment:

1. Identify the hazards
2. Identify the potential damage from each hazard

3. Evaluate the risks
4. Remove or control the major risks.

Hazards may come from the speaker, the speech, the audience, the hosts, the venue, the media or outside circumstances. To take a simple example, suppose you are speaking at a conference: one hazard might be the previous speaker, who has a reputation for over-running. The worst damage might be you are left with less than the allocated time. You evaluate the risk of that happening. Depending on how high the risk is, you could have a word with the organisers to find out how they would handle the situation, or be ready to make a short but still brilliant speech.

## If you invite someone to speak . . .

. . . you have a big part to play in the success of the occasion. It helps if you have a clear idea of the purpose of the speech. Make sure the speaker knows as much about you and your organisation as possible and is in touch with you or someone senior enough to discuss the content of the speech. Do offer suggestions. Ask what help you can provide. Be clear in writing about the arrangements, fee, expenses, press involvement and any task you would like the speaker to perform, such as presenting awards.

On the day, meet the speaker, look after them, their aides, and practicalities such as autocue and lighting. Use the occasion to get to know the speaker. A buffet or round-table meal will give you a better chance to do this than a top-table meal where the speaker talks only to the people on either side. If the speaker found the occasion worthwhile – and enjoyed themselves – they are more likely to accept a second invitation.

# Seven

# The speechwriter and the client

I am regularly told by people I meet on my training courses that writing a speech for someone else to deliver is, 'torture', 'terrifying', 'a waste of time, they'll only change it, so why bother?'. It is like making clothes without measurements and hoping they will fit. It is especially nerve-racking when the new clothes are for the emperor of your particular realm. But it is also curiously satisfying.

And there are a lot of speeches to write. If a hundred government ministers give, on average, just two speeches a week, that's ten thousand speeches a year. If the chairman and chief executive of Britain's thousand top companies give just one speech a week, that's a hundred thousand speeches a year. Nearly a million and a half conferences are held in Britain each year.[1] If each one has six speakers, that's 10 million speeches a year. Some busy speakers, such as cabinet ministers or executives of big organisations, may be on their feet five or ten times a week. A hidden army writes their speeches. Some are commissioned officers, others are unwilling conscripts, few have had any training.

## Why people have speechwriters

People employ speechwriters because they are too busy to do all the work themselves. They are also too tired. I hope they won't mind me saying this, but all the ministers I have ever worked with wear an ingrained tiredness from the demands of government routine. Naturally brilliant speakers use speechwriters to keep their speeches up to full strength. Less-talented speakers use a speechwriter to learn from. Keeping the CEO of a major corporation or a cabinet minister equipped with decent speeches is the best part of a full-time job.

There are three 'models' of speechwriting:

1. **White House** At the White House, speechwriters tend to work on words already on paper, crafting and refining the US President's speeches. The team is kept in seclusion. For reasons of security they may not be told the important parts of the speech; they are kept away from policy decisions. Peggy Noonan, Ronald Reagan's speechwriter, admits that she rarely met Reagan.[2]

2. **No. 10** For Tony Blair, officials at No. 10 contract out many speeches and articles to be ghostwritten, mainly by journalists, but they are finished by communications experts and policy advisers. No. 10 has been known to commission speeches from several writers and to choose the one nearest to its requirements. The speechwriters therefore have limited access to and influence on policy. They may know little of the workings of government. They may not be involved in the final stages of the drafting. They are anonymous.

3. **'Whitehall'** For most cabinet ministers, producing speeches is a collaborative process, involving them, policy officials, press advisers, political advisers, and a speechwriter, who may be one of the officials, a political adviser or someone else. The speechwriter is closely involved with the speaker and the policy at all stages. They

are as concerned with content and purpose as with style. They are anonymous. Many chief executives and directors in business and other non-government organisations use a similar process.

Which is best? The Whitehall model has the potential to produce the best speeches. The people involved understand the material and have access to it. They have political antennae. They are experts at what to say and when to say it. Because speechmaking is a collaborative process, there is some control over timing, and with big speeches the timing is crucial, like driving a lorry on to a busy roundabout. The speechwriter working in Whitehall, or in a similar setting, is closer to their speaker, the policy, the politics and the public than just about anyone else in the team. Civil servants are among the best speechwriters in the business.

You could, of course, call in a professional from a company specialising in speeches, but they won't know the speaker's style or policy, and they will cost a fortune. I would never advise contracting out something really important.

## What speechwriters do

The perfect speechwriter thinks about everything from the speaker's perspective. They understand the mind of the speaker so well that they can think like them and pre-empt the speaker's thinking. Their aim is twofold: to assist the speaker to give the best possible speech, and to make the process easy and, if possible, fun. Some speakers use speeches to test policy: the speechwriter is therefore involved in policy design. If something can be explained, in a speech, it will probably work in practice.

Michael Portillo recalled that it was 'a long and painful process' assisting Margaret Thatcher with her speeches. Her response to reading out his first attempt at a draft was an exasperated 'Can nobody write speeches?'[3] Matthew Parris said: 'I could put myself into John Major's skin. He does tend to drone, so I put in a section that could be droned.'[4] His client admitted that 'I find it hard to read speeches written by others . . . When I was prime minister my staff would often be in despair because they had produced a beautifully written speech that I would move around because they weren't all my own words.'[5] Overall the job of a speechwriter, as David Frum, a former speechwriter to George Bush, describes it, is 'to understand what the man is thinking'[6]

To be a speechwriter, you need a combination of two skills: a detailed knowledge of your client's subject – or the ability to grasp quickly any new mass of information – and the ability to put it across so that it is interesting and enjoyable to listen to. The latter is easier than the former. Your work is behind the scenes rather than in the spotlight. It is often an anonymous and always invisible profession. It helps if you like your speaker, because you will be working closely with them, and if you are a naturally good mimic. Speechwriting is akin to ghostwriting or parody. If you do any of these things well you can probably hear your speaker's voice in your mind. Not everyone can.

You may have one further role as a speechwriter, and that is in assisting your speaker to decide whether and when to make speeches. Some are so keen for publicity that they accept any and all speaking invitations. They end up on a merry-go-round of appearances at minor occasions, leaving no time for more important ones. As their speechwriter, you may be able to suggest that they focus a little more strategically on their speeches. All senior speakers should have a speaking strategy as part of their overall communication plan, maybe looking a year ahead to map out the main speaking and statement occasions, and, if necessary, creating opportunities to speak.

## Do you need a speechwriter?

If you give more than a dozen or so big speeches each year, consider organising some assistance with them. You may not want or need a full-time professional writer but you could probably use some help with the research, drafting, organising, managing and rehearsing, and in developing your style. Even with a speechwriter you will probably work just as hard on your speeches. No good speaker takes a draft without improving it and making it their own. All the ministers I have worked with spend two days before a major speech working on little else, sometimes after months of preparation.

Some speechwriters are journalists, press and publicity professionals, others are in external relations, strategy, finance or operations. Special advisers, executive assistants, secretaries, partners and families help with speeches – Bill Clinton would get Hillary to assist him with his presidential speeches. As less than 10 per cent of speech preparation is in the writing, wordsmithing isn't the main requirement. Some of the best speechwriters I know are analysts and finance directors, who have a grasp of the big picture and can present logical, reasonable, persuasive, well-supported arguments. Skill with a calculator is as important as literary genius, and this, of course, is where some professional speechwriters or those hired in for their dramatic ability reach their limits. The big speech requires a deep and up-to-the-minute understanding of the subject, and of the context in which it will be delivered. The ability to sense mood and reflect it in words cannot be bought or bolted on.

Someone somewhere in your organisation will be able to do this job, and it may not be the person you expect. You will probably start by looking at your press officers, marketing people, special advisers, or in the PR, education, sales, publications, advertising or webmaster department, or wherever the jobs require skill in communication. Some people may write well, but their specialist skill may be different from what you need. Press officers are often journalists who write clearly and at great speed, but few enjoy writing speeches: they tend to find big speeches agonisingly boring compared with fast news stories. They are often dissatisfied with what they produce, because their usual style of writing and speaking – with all the interesting material packed into the beginning and getting less interesting towards the end – is perfect for media purposes but unbalanced for a speech.

The person who does a lot of public speaking, the natural comic or the life and soul of the office party, may not be a good speechwriter. Very often those who write to express their own thoughts don't enjoy writing for others; in the same way, while some composers are also performers of music, many aren't. Those who like to write for others are not always speakers.

Speeches are a great leveller of the work hierarchy: the ability to write a good speech does not necessarily improve with rank. Seniority sometimes stifles flair. Often it is the quietest people in an organisation who have a natural gift for speechwriting. One of the best natural talents I came across among people I have trained was a quietly spoken man in a junior grade who was so shy that he was unable to read aloud his or anyone else's script. Yet his speeches for others were magnificent. So, look beyond the obvious candidates.

Your speechwriter must be someone who knows you – or someone you don't mind getting to know you well. One cabinet minister told me that writing speeches for him was the worst job in the world and his wife agreed. Speeches don't confine themselves to the office. You have to work with someone in a close relationship: neither of you knows where you are heading at the start of a speech; 90 per cent of the work you do may be discarded; and much of it takes place at night.

Give any likely contender the chance to have a go. The first speech they write for you is as much about the process as the product: you need someone who can make it easy and fun for you as they find out how you like to work and what you find helpful. By speech two or three, you will have a good idea if you can work together.

Make it clear that the script is between you and the writer: a manager will be behind your probationer speechwriter, ready to remove from it all trace of excitement and, with it, the risk that it may reflect badly on them. Managers may not care how dull a speech is, as long as there are no fires to put out later. You, on the other hand, want an interesting speech, good enough to set the world alight. Your probationer may need to be shielded from their superiors.

## The process of writing a speech

It is hardly surprising that so many speeches fail when we consider how they were put together. Here is an imaginary scenario. You receive in the post a polite invitation to speak, as last year, at the annual conference for the UK Widget Makers Association. You answer on a first-come-first-served basis, and enter it in the diary. Two weeks before the event, you ask someone to prepare a speech, offering no brief; the person you ask has no training, and is ill-equipped for the task. A draft yo-yos up and down the chain of command (this happens a lot in the civil service). Everyone thinks someone else will do the necessary research, but no one does. The most junior person comes up with a few familiar lines: they have never met the speaker and have no idea of their style. The first thing the speaker sees is an unreadable draft, and realises they have more pressing things to attend to. They delegate delivery of the speech to someone else. Speaker number two has a second-hand draft and no time to prepare except on the way to the event. They emerge from the car with twenty questions and no answers, then discover that the writer isn't there. But the audience is. The speaker steps on to the podium. He's a little late, but still has fifteen minutes to fill with a ten-minute speech. He begins to speak . . .

At this point one of two things may happen. Either the speaker reads the speech verbatim. Or they busk. Either way, someone is going to be unhappy. The conference organisers feel snubbed because they have had to accept a substitute speaker. The audience, unless the busking is good, receives the speech coolly. The speaker and the audience agree on one point: that their time could have been better spent.

The journalists, less than impressed, make a mental note to give that speaker a miss next time. There are no copies of the speech available for them to find even a shred of news for their story, so they jot down some off-the-cuff comments and write their copy. The following day, the speaker's unguarded, unscripted comments are in a national newspaper.

The speaker spends the following week trying to make amends.

It is rarely quite so bad, but it is by this process that, week in week out, captive audiences at conferences and other events hear some rotten speeches. And if one thing goes wrong, several others will. A chief executive said to me, 'They see me busk and they think that because I'm good at it I enjoy it. I don't. There is nothing worse than realising the draft in your hand is no good. If I had better drafts I'd give them. But I don't have time . . .' Every speaker has painful memories of a speech that went wrong.

To avoid this happening, ensure that:
- The draft is commissioned in good time
- The writer anticipates that a speech will be required
- The speaker gives guidance on how they like their speeches. Well-prepared speakers produce written guidance notes.

- The speaker allows enough time for preparation
- One person is the point of contact to manage the speech, drawing in expertise at all levels as required
- The writer and speaker meet
- The writer has some aptitude or training for speeches
- The writer makes sure that all possible lines of research are carried out
- The first thing the speaker sees is a reasonable outline, with options, and as much background research as can be mustered.

It would be comforting to say that it is easier to do a speech well than badly, but that's not so. A reasonable speech requires a lot of effort, even with a speechwriter, but the rewards are incomparable.

## Why it takes three weeks to put together a good impromptu speech

Mark Twain said: 'It takes three weeks to make a good impromptu speech.' He was right. The following table shows the processes involved in preparing a moderately important speech for, say, a policy announcement or major conference. The really big speeches such as a chancellor's budget speech take even more time, so:

- only do them if it's worth it
- if you are the speaker get as much help as you can.

**Why it takes three weeks to write a good impromptu speech**

| | Time (hours) | |
|---|---|---|
| WEEK 1 | Support | Speaker |
| **Invitation** Ask for advice on whether the invitation should be accepted. Be clear about what the speaker and the organisation want to achieve. Decide on response. Reply to invitation. | 5 | 1 |
| **Research** the audience, the occasion, the subject. Work out and circulate a timetable. Brief all involved. | 10 | 0 |
| **Content** Develop the theme and main points of the speech. Commission/write contributions. | 10 | 0 |
| **Outline** Prepare and agree an outline speech. Decide on a structure. | 5 | 4 |
| WEEK 2 | | |
| **First draft** Write and word-process the draft. Clear it. Further research on content. Chase contributions. Redraft. Prepare an attention-grabbing introduction. | 30 | 5 |

| WEEK 3 | Support | Speaker |
|---|---|---|
| **Final drafts**  Further drafting and research. Final checks for accuracy, clarity Prepare a resounding conclusion. | 10 | 7 |
| **Finishing touches**  Memorise the first few sentences. Rehearse. Practise dealing with questions. Prepare a final, readable script. Make copies. Distribute any advance copies. | 10 | 5 |
| **Deliver the speech**  Travel. Attend the occasion. Circulate script. Listen to other speeches. | 5 | 5 |
| **Afterwards**  Media interviews. Respond to reactions. | 5 | 3 |
| **Total** | **90** | **30** |

**120 hours**

**i.e., three weeks**

## Guidance on speaker's preferences

If you have someone to assist you with your speeches, and especially if different people help on different speeches, you will make their lives easier by offering them guidance in advance on your preferences. One minister I know supplies six pages of notes.

## Getting to know your speaker

Most speakers are happy to share what works for them, so ask them. Here are some questions I have found useful in getting a discussion going:

- What instructions would you give someone drafting a speech for you?
- What are you looking for in a good speech?
- What works best for you?
- What don't you like about the drafts coming to you now?
- How can I best help you prepare for a speech?
- What would you say was your most successful speech, and why?
- Do you have copies of speeches that have gone well?
- What made those speeches go well?
- Do you prefer to speak from a draft or to appear off-the-cuff?
- What are you hoping to achieve with your next few speeches?
- Are there any speaking opportunities I should look out for?
- What are the most important audiences to you?
- What's the biggest success you want to achieve with a speech?

Some questions you can't put to your speaker, so ask someone else who will know the answer. Secretaries know how their boss works, in detail, like what sort of last-minute changes they make, if the process is solitary or done by committee, what type of assistance they most value, what annoys and makes them nervous. Videos of speeches are a real prize: they can show the speaker's style, the language they use, their speed of delivery, etc.

It's not hard to find out about their background, interests and family – and the extent to which they reveal them in public. Specialist interest should be cautiously applied. A chairman of a British financial institution liked to use his speeches to show off his knowledge of military history and selected a speechwriter with the same interest. What he should have been doing was demonstrating his institution's ability to compete in a tough global marketplace. One private secretary judges the success of his boss's speeches from the amount of time devoted in the speech to his hobby, fishing. The more mention of fishing, the worse the draft and the more the speaker improvises . . . Some speakers are scholars in their own right. Former culture secretary Chris Smith is a Wordsworth scholar (and currently chairman of the Wordsworth Trust) and linked Wordsworth's love of nature with government policy on countryside access in a way that rendered a speechwriter superfluous.

I said earlier that speechwriting is akin to parody and you can have fun scribbling in different styles. Here is Winston Churchill's 'finest hour' speech, of 18 June 1940, adapted to the style of Tony Blair around 1997:

> *After* 'la guerre de Gaulle', *now the Battle for Britain. The power, the glory, for ever and ever. For Britain. But I am not complacent. It is not inconceivable that our enemies may soon attack. I do not want our country to sink into a night made only darker by the deeds of evil men. I want the whole world to rise into a new dawn in which the people of Britain are the brightest lights. If we fail, New Britannia will be as if she had never been. It is time for action. Time for Britain to be nothing*

*less than the model nation for the next millennium, from where our children will look back and say 'Actually, you know, they did it OK.'*

What Churchill really said was:

*What General Weygand called the Battle of France is over. I expect that the Battle of Britain is about to begin. Upon this battle depends the survival of Christian civilisation. Upon it depends our own British life, and the long continuity of our institutions and our Empire. The whole fury and might of the enemy must very soon be turned on us. Hitler knows that he will have to break us in this island or lose the war. If we can stand up to him, all Europe may be free and the life of the world may move forward into broad sunlit uplands. But if we fail, then the whole world, including the United States, including all that we have known and cared for, will sink into the abyss of a new Dark Age made more sinister, and perhaps more protracted, by the lights of perverted science. Let us therefore brace ourselves to our duties and so bear ourselves that, if the British Empire and its Commonwealth last for a thousand years, men will still say, 'This was their finest hour.'* [7]

## A message from a speaker to their speechwriter

If I had to put together everything speakers have told me they want from a speechwriter it would say something like this:

*Think first about the objective of the speech – what do I really want to achieve? What is possible? What is the news value? What is the business value? Should I be doing the speech at all?*

*Then I want a good thesis. I prefer wit and lightness of touch to jokes. I don't want jargon. I want good clear English. Above all, I want something that is sayable, that sounds human and as though I had written it myself. But please don't think that if I change your draft it means it was no good – on the contrary, it was helpful and my rewriting helps me to take over the speech and for it to belong to me. Writing it out again in different words is my way of learning my lines, of getting into it. I still get nervous before a major speech, so I appreciate thorough briefing. I know you want a cleared draft well in advance, but be patient, this speech has to hit exactly the right spot at the right time, so last-minute adjustments may be unavoidable.*

If you are a senior figure, you might add, 'Please remember, I want a speech suitable for a secretary of state/director/CEO. If you could give this speech yourself, as a civil servant/manager, it is the wrong speech.'

What they won't say, but what you the speechwriter should aim for above all else, is a speech that enhances the speaker's reputation.

## A message from a speechwriter to a speaker

And what all speechwriters would like to say to their speakers:

*I'll try and make your speeches more eloquent but I'm more interested in making them work, to make the process comfortable, and for you to get the best possible response from the audience. You probably thought that hiring me would mean that you wouldn't have to spend so much time on your speeches. I will, of course, save you time, but no one can write a truly great speech for someone else. The bigger the speech, the more*

*time I guess you will need to spend working on it yourself.
Those around you will be pressing you for the draft in advance
of the performance, but I know the importance of last-minute
drafting. I know how important it is to be fresh and topical so I
will protect you as best I can from having the draft snatched
away before you have finished with it. Please tell me how the
speech went. I learn only from feedback. And come the day
when you say my words 'sounded just like me' I'll know I'm
doing something right.*

I can't resist including some advice on speeches from a work of
fiction – or was it autobiography? *A Parliamentary Affair*, by Edwina
Currie, tells the story of a liaison between two MPs, the junior but
ambitious Elaine, and the senior, cautious Roger. In this extract,
Elaine is coaching Roger:

*'. . . Decide first what message you want to get across: if it's
important, keep saying it in the same words, over and over
again.' . . . Then: 'All speeches are composed of three things:
message, medium and mode. Message we've done. By 'medium' I
mean you must know who the audience is and exactly what are
the circumstances. Are you speaking live or recorded? First or
last? Live is always best as you can't be edited and if you're
determined enough you can get the last word in . . . Try out
your expression in front of a mirror. Listen to your own voice –
practise with a tape-recorder. Learn what it sounds like, and
how to make it sing.'*
*'Yes,' he admitted slowly. 'My voice always sounds so flat and
toneless. I'll try that.'*
*She nodded, content. 'Lastly is the mode, by which I mean you
should back up your message with real knowledge and not*

*waffle. Always be well prepared. If you make a point, have some evidence. A few well-chosen facts will stick.'* [8]

## From one speechwriter to another . . .

You've left no stone unturned in researching a speech, you've written it so that no one will ever guess it is anything other than the speaker's own handiwork, you've done what you can to avoid any nasty surprises from the audience or from the technology, you've told the world to expect a great speech. The moment the speaker steps onto the podium, they are on their own. There is nothing more you can do to help them.

# Eight

# Giving and receiving a speech

Effective speakers pay less attention than many would imagine to the way they perform. The inexperienced tend to say: 'It's all in the way people deliver speeches – the tone of voice, the way they act, pauses, hand movements, body movements, dressing for effect, timing, talking through applause . . . They're trained or they are just good at that sort of thing . . .' Their perception seems to be that a polished performance is the sole determinant of success, that making a speech is more about delivery than content, so they focus on themselves and their performance, perhaps with help from a trainer or coach.

But all the help in the world is no guarantee that a speech will be well received, so the terror of public speaking never goes away. If help is not available, the inexperienced speaker may think that they cannot perform adequately and give up trying. All speakers get nervous, especially on big occasions, but the experienced get round this by focusing on the audience and on the content of their speech, which gives them confidence. This doesn't mean that performance isn't important. In this chapter we will look at how to put the finishing touches to a speech and how to deliver it so that you get the reception you deserve.

## Voice

A speaker probably doesn't need to give too much attention to improving their voice. If a voice is authentic, sincere and loud enough to be heard, accents and individual mannerisms don't matter to audiences and may be an advantage. It's just a question of making the most of what Nature provided. Relax, and don't forget to breathe.

The voices we most like to hear delivering speeches are distinctive, often to the point of being odd – like Churchill's rumbling war roar or Tony Benn's rolling growl. Their individuality is not a hindrance, but a strength. Benn and Churchill's voices seem to resonate from deep within the speaker.

No speaker I have worked with has undergone voice training, as far as I am aware, but there are a few problems with which it may be useful to have professional help. Women with high-pitched voices may sound shrill, and need to learn how to make their voices carry. It is well known that Margaret Thatcher received professional help to drop the pitch of her voice, and so did Diana, Princess of Wales. On the other hand, a woman's voice may have a broader tonal range than a man's and more natural musicality. Some voices can be irritating, and only self-awareness will tell you if that might include yours. If you consider that voice training might help you or your speaker then plenty of help is available, from professional voice coaches to amateur dramatic groups.

## Body language

The perceived wisdom is to stand still, knees relaxed, hands by the sides. Have you tried doing that for more than two minutes? It's impossible for some of us. Who cares if a speaker uses their hands or moves around? Audiences may prefer it as evidence that the speaker is human – it may even help to get the message across. The words of those who talk with their hands are more likely to be remembered accurately than those of people who merely talk.[1] When a speaker uses gestures as well as speech, the listener is less likely to change the story in retelling it. If the speaker is thinking hard about what they are saying they cut down on body gestures – which is what people do when they are lying. So contrived body language may be interpreted by the audience as a sign that the speaker is not being truthful.[2] If we want to increase trust through speeches, body language must inspire it. So it must be genuine: relax and be yourself. If your facial expressions naturally reflect your words and the mood of what you are saying, you and others like you, such as Bill Clinton, have an advantage over the rest of us.

Of course, if you habitually jangle your keys, fiddle with cufflinks, wag a finger, it might detract from your performance: such gestures, known as emotional leakage, dissipate rather than concentrate a message. The solution may be to work a little harder in finding words that say exactly what you mean.

There are only two situations in which body language is a problem. The first is when the words delivered are more a presentation or commentary, in which case gestures detract from the visual focus of attention. The second is when body language says one thing but the words say another. In his speech as health secretary at the 1999 Labour Party Conference, Alan Milburn leant forward and jabbed a finger over the lectern, chin up and out. His body language was aggressive, threatening. In fact, he was announcing more money for hospices. Confused by the mismatch between the threatening body language and welcome good news, the delegates were unsure how to respond and their applause was lukewarm.

## Acting the part?

Body language is subtle, unconscious, and cannot be altered without training. A speaker delivering a big speech has more important things to think about than their voice and their actions. Speakers aren't actors. A poor speech delivered by a brilliant actor will still be a poor speech. It is more important to get the content right, to say what you mean, and mean what you say, than to act. The rhetorical devices described on pages 42-45 are far more reliable in generating positive audience reaction than acting skills. We often hear that politicians and royalty have been advised by actors, but unless an actor can understand and interpret their client's subject matter, the benefits of this are limited. The Conservative Party was reported to have spent £100,000 on teaching Iain Duncan Smith to 'walk, talk and look the part'.[3] Was the money well spent? Too much coaching may produce a performance so polished that all the audience sees is the reflection. A little coaching may not be enough to change the habits of a lifetime and the speaker may appear self-consciously robotic.

Most speakers make do with their natural talents. High-profile speakers learn from seeing themselves on television. The rest of us can improve by watching videos of ourselves and from honest feedback.

## Props

As discussed in chapter 1, speeches are not presentations and speakers seldom use props or visual aids. Yet the less experienced the speaker, the more likely they are to rely on a Powerpoint presentation or slides. Then more effort goes into grappling with the computer than into the content of the speech. The argument for having visuals relates to the theory that we remember a small fraction of what we hear, a small fraction of what we see, but a large fraction of what we see and hear. When a speech is to be delivered, the audience comes to see the speaker. Make life easy: do speeches, not presentations! You can deliver a speech even if the organisers are unprepared, the technology doesn't work, or there is a power-cut. Your presence is the best visual aid the audience could hope for.

But props are sometimes unavoidable. I was involved in preparations for John Major's last major policy announcement before the 1997 general election. The proposals – to introduce a funded state pension scheme – were complex and we chose to have a multi-media announcement presentation, the first, as far as I am aware, by a prime minister. It took a year to plan, two sets of technology and technicians, in case of breakdowns, and careful rehearsal. The launch went without a hitch, although the policy received a mauling from Labour in the run-up to the election. Think carefully about whether the time you invest in technology is worth while.

If you like to use pictures, make sure that they tell the story, with the words as a commentary – Colin Powell did this when he addressed the UN Security Council in February 2003:

> *At this ballistic missile site, on November 10, we saw a cargo truck preparing to move ballistic missile components. At this biological weapons related facility, on November 25, just two days before inspections resumed, this truck caravan appeared, something we almost never see at this facility, and we monitor it carefully and regularly. At this ballistic missile facility, again, two days before inspections began, five large cargo trucks appeared along with the truck-mounted crane to move missiles. We saw this kind of house cleaning at close to thirty sites. Days after this activity, the vehicles and the equipment that I've just*

*highlighted disappear and the site returns to patterns of normalcy.*[4]

It was a powerful presentation, piecing together the intelligence evidence for weapons of mass destruction in Iraq from an overwhelming mass of detail. Powell spoke the above passage relatively early in the presentation, and was instantly convincing, setting the tone for what followed. However, the presentation was so lengthy that perhaps the inadequacy of much of the later evidence, based on a handful of witnesses and artistic reconstructions rather than photographs, was overlooked:

> *A third source, also in a position to know, reported in summer 2002 that Iraq had manufactured mobile production systems mounted on road trailer units and on rail cars. Finally, a fourth source, an Iraqi major, who defected, confirmed that Iraq has mobile biological research laboratories, in addition to the production facilities I mentioned earlier. We have diagrammed what our sources reported about these mobile facilities. Here you see both truck and rail car-mounted mobile factories. The description our sources gave us of the technical features required by such facilities is highly detailed and extremely accurate. As these drawings based on their description show, we know what the fermenters look like, we know what the tanks, pumps, compressors and other parts look like. We know how they fit together. We know how they work. And we know a great deal about the platforms on which they are mounted. As shown in this diagram, these factories can be concealed easily, either by moving ordinary-looking trucks and rail cars along Iraq's thousands of miles of highway or track, or by parking them in a garage or warehouse or somewhere in Iraq's extensive system of underground tunnels and bunkers.*

## Appearance

So, voice, body language and props don't much matter. But appearance does. We all know that first impressions count and that an audience makes its judgement a few seconds after the speaker has begun. The first assessment we make on meeting someone is about gender – apparently it is of prime importance to us to know if someone we meet is male or female. Then we make a rough assessment of age, and from a combination of other clues, a series of judgements about the speaker's status, competence and attractiveness. Appearance is part of the visual jargon, telling the audience, as we saw in chapter 3 (pages 66-67), which 'club' the speaker belongs to, their status and effectiveness within it, and whether it's the same club as ours. Assuming that gender, age, race/culture are givens, the only variable in which a speaker has much choice is dress.

An honest appraisal of appearance, clothes and grooming can be a great confidence boost. Most women feel less anxious when they are happy with their clothes and hair. In most men, their only anxiety, I am told, is whether their flies are undone.

If you feel image isn't important and that you can compensate for any deficiencies with the brilliance of your speech, then that is fine, but it adds to the burden of preparing the content. Sometimes the clothes eclipse the content, as happened to Tony Blair at the 2000 Labour Party Conference when the main talking-point afterwards was his sweat-soaked shirt. Teresa May's girls'-night-out shoes stole the show at the 2002 Conservative Party Conference.

## Stage fright

Even the most experienced speakers are nervous before a speech. And the perceived wisdom on dealing with stage fright isn't always helpful. A book on speeches published as recently as 1998,[5] advises a speaker to: 'Get a grip on yourself.'

The genuinely terrified can try deep-breathing exercises, but the best approach is to work out what the terror relates to. Then it will seem less important. Fear of a hostile reaction is common, but can be reduced by audience research. It is usually possible to make discreet enquiries in advance about what audience reaction is likely to be and address it. Fear of the unknown is also common: again, research is helpful. Find out as much as possible about the event, do everything possible to avoid surprises. On the way to the podium, do everything in slow motion. When we are stressed, we rush so that we can get away from the upsetting situation. If you slow down you will have a chance to look around, size up the situation, discover that maybe it isn't as terrifying as it appears, then take control of it.

During a speech, the speaker may be able to ask the audience questions. If he or she asks about their experiences – even if only for a show of hands – they will gain information, and the audience will feel it has been consulted. But a speaker's best defence against stage fright is confidence in what they have to say.

## Rehearsal

All good speakers rehearse. George Bush underwent four full dress rehearsals for his 2003 State of the Union address.[6]

### How to get the best out of a rehearsal:

**As the speaker**, you should enlist the best help available: line up your experts, advisers, secretary, family and brief them on what they are to do. Don't ask 'How was my speech?' because people are generally too polite to say anything discouraging – conversely, if they say something you don't want to hear, you won't hear it. They may say something too vague to act upon – the favourite is 'needs to be more punchy'. Take control of the rehearsal: instruct your volunteer audience on the sort of feedback you want:

- Can you hear me?
- What do the audience like most?
- What needs cutting out?
- What's missing?
- Is the main argument clear?
- How's the beginning?
- Where's the best point for a cheer?

**As the speechwriter**, you should make the process comfortable and fun. Your speaker is probably at their most fractious, so this is a time for pandering to their every whim, and finding a solution to every problem. Your first task is to set up the rehearsal with a real or improvised lectern. If your speaker is a front-bencher and the occasion a parliamentary one, a couple of ministerial red boxes on a table will serve as the dispatch box, with a row of chairs lined up as the opposition front bench. Every speaker needs different support, but here, in no particular order, are some of the tasks you may face:

- Filter advice and comments
- Draft tricky sections
- Draft any extra sections you anticipate may be needed
- Find the speaker's spectacles
- Maintain endless supply of tea or coffee (serious speakers seldom use alcohol)
- Keep the press notice in line with the speech

- Keep hold of and be able to find any relevant papers
- Negotiate clearance of draft
- Keep speaker's file up to date
- Type
- Alert press office to any new drafting that might be newsworthy
- Fiddle with main soundbites
- Send home for that all-important page left on hall table
- Have ink for favourite pen
- Produce black tie
- Count the words
- Keep an eye on unfolding news and report back
- Locate the toilets
- Keep an eye on the time
- Keep away any distractions

## How many words?

You will almost certainly need to check that the speech is the right length. About 120 words per minute seems to be the average, so a five-minute speech is around 600 words, 10 minutes is 1200, 15 minutes is 1800, 20 minutes is 2400. It does, however, vary from person to person and from place to place. A speech would take longer to deliver at a formal occasion in a large hall than at an informal gathering. Below 90 words a minute is too slow and over 140 too fast. A stopwatch is handy.

## Is this a good speech?

**Content**

1. Is there a clear, new idea?

2. Will it meet its purpose?

**Speaker**

1. Does it convey with confidence what the speaker thinks, feels and knows?

2. Does it match the speaker's style?

3. Will it enhance the speaker's reputation?

4. Is the speaker happy with it?

5. Is it sayable?

**Structure**

1. Does the beginning grab the attention?

2. Does it avoid sticking to the 'middle ground'?

3. Are there memorable phrases?

4. Does it end on a positive?

**Audience**

1. Is there something in it for all members of the audience?

2. Does it contain the right cues for the responses you want from the audience?

3. Does it provide a service for the audience?

4. Is it easy to listen to?

**Practicalities**

1. Is it the right length?

2. Is the speaker's draft secure and readable?

3. Is the venue prepared and the technology (microphone, etc.) working?

4. Is there a press release or article?

## Finishing touches

By now the draft will be nearing completion and will need a final check. Is it a good speech? The table on page 156 supplies a checklist of questions about the content and structure of the draft, the main priorities for the speaker and the audience, and essential practicalities. If the answer to all of these questions is 'yes', you have a good speech. If any produce 'no', you will be able to identify the areas that need more work.

## First aid

There never seems to be enough time to draft a perfect speech. When preparation time is limited, the following suggestions may help:

1. '**Get the ducks lined up**' The priority is the right content, which must meet the needs of speaker, audience and occasion.
2. **Check it is sayable** If the speaker is using a full draft, every word must be sayable, acronyms known, pronunciation decided, figures and diagrams interpreted in words.
3. **Paint a picture, tell a story** Imagery makes speeches memorable (see page 43). Introducing imagery into a speech will make perhaps the biggest single improvement.
4. **Draft a quote for the press**
5. **Rehearse**
6. **Learn the beginning by heart**.

This list is also useful as a final check for speeches on which so much work has been done that something important may have been overlooked.

## The 'good-enough' speech

For most occasions, even big ones, a speech does not have to be sensational or brilliant. A 'good-enough' speech concentrates on what's interesting, pitches the content at the right level, isn't out of place compared with local or organisational norms, but is just that bit better than the audience might have expected. Almost anyone can produce a good-enough speech that's appropriate to the occasion and the speaker, that will hold people's interest and put across its message clearly and simply.

## The script

Should you speak from a script or without notes? Most people start out preferring one or the other, but when the engagements become more important, it is hard to get by without a script. With more experience, it becomes possible to deliver a bigger speech without a script, but there always seems to be an occasion round the corner when only a full written text of the speech will do. Sometimes every word counts. Colin Powell's speech to the UN Security Council (see page 150) would have been impossible to deliver without a full script.

On informal occasions, try to manage without notes. Keep the speech to a handful of points.

**SCRIPT OR NO SCRIPT?**

|      | No script | Script |
|------|-----------|--------|
| **Pros** | Looks spontaneous<br>Informal<br>Can hold audience attention with eyes<br>Can see audience and gauge reaction<br>May sound more like a conversation<br>Audience may interpret it as sincere | Well crafted<br>Can be given in advance to the press<br>Looks professional<br>Audience may interpret it as more prepared<br>Audience may interpret it as more respectful. |
| **Cons** | Not formal enough<br>Difficult to get structure and wording working as well as they might<br>Impossible when accuracy needed, e.g. in statements to Parliament<br>Less likely to be accurately quoted or quoted at all<br>Audience may interpret it as unprepared | Too formal<br>Reading from a script may be frowned on, e.g. in Parliament where technically should speak only from notes, not a full script<br>Audience may interpret it as not spontaneous enough |

## Speaking without a script

The course of at least two recent general election campaigns changed when the future prime ministers threw away their scripts and spoke off the cuff. In 1992, frustrated by his failure to find a means of communicating, John Major turned up at a rally in Luton with a packing case and a loudhailer. Later he explained,

> *'I learned my politics on a soapbox in Brixton. I feel at home, I don't like speaking to an audience on a platform, the audience*

*seated down there at a distance . . . there is no contact, no
humanity, no relationship. So I was looking to get on a soapbox
all the time. People kept saying "No, you mustn't do it, too
dangerous, won't work, not prime ministerial." Eventually,
events pushed us in that direction and I just did it.*[7]

It wasn't a complete success: the Socialist Worker's Party had a bigger
loudhailer and Major was forced to retreat. The press sneered. In
spite of his failure, for Major it was a liberation. Anthony Seldon
described him as 'rejuvenated . . . Uniquely himself and in
command of his destiny.'[7]

At a rally in 1997, when Tony Blair's microphone failed, he threw
it down with his script and carried on impromptu. The crowd loved
it. For Blair it was a one-off: he prefers mostly to stick to a prepared
script on larger occasions.

Ann Widdecombe, as shadow health secretary at the 1998
Conservative Party Conference, delivered her entire speech
without a script, demanding the return of hospital matrons.
Looking and sounding not unlike one herself in a blue suit and
white collar, she declaimed: 'She was a dragon and she was a
champion and we want her BACK!'[8] She had been a minister since
1992 and so was already an experienced speaker, but in opposition
after 1997 she had more freedom to experiment and her 1998
speech defined her style.

It isn't a good idea to learn a speech by heart – it's more or less
impossible for most of us anyway. Here's a useful tip: to commit the
outline of a speech to memory, imagine a journey. If the speech will
last five minutes, imagine a familiar five-minute journey – say, the
drive from the office to the station. Link places along the journey
with different parts of the speech and add a few objects along the
way to act as landmarks – the more incongruous the better. For

example, the cue for the section about the environmental impact of a policy might be your arrival at a pillarbox, which, in your mind's eye, is bright green.

Speaking with notes often results in the dry, flavourless speech that audiences dread. What you say won't sound like a speech because the words won't have been crafted to read like one and will sound like headings. Imagine Martin Luther King's 'I have a dream' speech as a list of bullet points.

The popular solution, a handful of cards, looks amateurish and fiddly to me. You can get by with notes if, for example, you have given a similar speech before and just need a few prompts: then have the outline mapped out on a single piece of paper. Margaret Thatcher wrote the notes for her Francis of Assisi speech, which she read before entering 10 Downing Street for the first time in 1979, on a tiny card that she held in the palm of her hand.[9]

## Sample layouts

The layout of a script is a matter of personal preference. Use a typeface you can read easily and make sure that the point size is large enough but not unwieldy. Some speakers go through their scripts marking extra punctuation for pauses, emphasis, where the intonation should go up, where to go down, etc. Punctuation was invented about 2200 years ago as a system of dramatic notation, signalling when actors should breathe. That was its main use for 1500 years. So we might think that punctuation would be just the thing to improve a speech. But there are disadvantages in punctuating a script. First, marking up a draft takes time. Second, most speakers find a marked-up draft difficult to read and it sounds stilted. Third, it looks unprofessional, and journalists may poke fun at it. Fourth, over a few hundred years punctuation has become more complicated: if you read a sign (it exists somewhere in Africa) that says 'CROCODILES DO NOT SWIM HERE' would you get into the water? It depends on the punctuation after the word 'crocodiles'. Try writing your draft with as little punctuation as possible, using only full stops, commas and dashes. Let the natural rhythms of the words help you with punctuation and intonation.

Here are four possible formats, each of which is useful on occasion:

1. **Minimal punctuation** Useful at draft stage to check the flow.
2. **Double spaced** Useful at draft stage: plenty of room for manuscript revisions. Poor as a script: too easy to skip a line because of the wide gaps.
3. **Chunked text** Each sentence is set on a separate line. It is easy to read out loud and is useful for checking phrasing. You can also spot any overlong sentences. This is a luxury script, which takes time to prepare and space to lay it out, and may not be suitable for distribution copies. When the Church of England introduced the new Prayer Book in the 1960s, it used chunked text for all the prayers, which made them easier to read out although it increased the size of the book.
4. **Times roman 14-point, single spaced, one sentence per paragraph** works well for most speakers. Some speakers like to restrict the words to the top half of the page so they don't have to look down too much.

To illustrate these layouts here are sections of four fine speeches charting some of the Northern Ireland peace process.

## 1 Minimal punctuation

What we democratic politicians want in Northern Ireland is a normal society. The best way to secure that normalcy is the tried and trusted method of parliamentary democracy. Burke said it best. 'Parliament is not a congress of ambassadors from different and hostile interests which interests each must maintain, as an agent and an advocate, against other agents and advocates but Parliament is a deliberative assembly of one nation, with one interest that of the whole where not local purposes, nor local prejudices ought to guide, but the general good resulting from the general reason of the whole.' Some critics complain that I lack 'the vision thing'. But vision in its pure meaning is clear sight. That does not mean I have no dreams. I do. But I try to have them at night. By day I am satisfied if I can see the furthest limit of what is possible. Politics can be likened to driving at night over unfamiliar hills and mountains. Close attention must be paid to what the beam can reach and the next bend. Driving by day as I believe we are now doing we should drive steadily not recklessly studying the countryside ahead with judicious glances in the mirror. We should be encouraged by having come so far and face into the next hill rather than the mountain beyond. It is not that the mountain is not in my mind but the hill has to be climbed first. There are hills in Northern Ireland and there are mountains. The hills are decommissioning and policing. But the mountain if we could but see it clearly is not in front of us but behind us in history. The dark shadow we seem to see in the distance is not really a mountain ahead but the shadow of the mountain behind. A shadow from the past thrown forward into our future. It is a dark sludge of historical sectarianism. We can leave it behind

*David Trimble, Nobel Lecture, Oslo, 10 December 1998*

## 2 Double spaced

Difficult, sometimes wrenching decisions lie ahead, but they must

be made. And because you have agreed to share responsibilities,

whenever possible you must try to act in concert, not conflict; to

overcome obstacles, not create them; to rise above petty disputes,

not fuel them.

The Latin word for assembly, 'concilium', is the root of the word

'reconciliation'. The spirit of reconciliation must be rooted in all

you do.

There is another quality you will need, too. Our only Irish

Catholic president, John Kennedy, loved to quote a certain British

Protestant prime minister. 'Courage,' Winston Churchill said, 'is

rightly esteemed as the first of all qualities because it is the quality

that guarantees all the others.'

Courage and reconciliation were the heart of your commitment to

peace. Now, as you go forward, courage and reconciliation must drive this Assembly in very specific ways: to decommission the weapons of war that are obsolete in Northern Ireland at peace; to move forward with the formation of an executive council; to adapt your police force so that it earns the confidence, respect and support of all the people; to end street justice, because defining crime, applying punishment and enforcing the law must be left to the people's elected representatives, the courts and the police; to pursue early release for prisoners whose organisations have truly abandoned violence, and to help them find a productive, constructive place in society; to build a more just society where human rights are birthrights and where every citizen receives equal protection and equal treatment under the law. These must be the benchmarks of the new Northern Ireland.

*President Clinton to the Northern Ireland Assembly,*
*The Waterfront Hall, Belfast, 3 September 1998*

### 3 Chunked text

But the crunch is the crunch.
There is no parallel track left.
The fork in the road has finally come.
Whatever guarantees we need to give that we will implement the
Agreement,
we will.
Whatever commitment to the end we all want to see,
of a normalised Northern Ireland,
I will make.


But we cannot carry on with the IRA half in,
half out of this process.
Not just because it isn't right any more.
It won't work any more.


Remove the threat of violence and the peace process is on an
unstoppable path.
That threat, no matter how damped down,
is no longer reinforcing the political,
it is actually destroying it.


In fact, the continuing existence of the IRA as an active paramil-
itary organisation is now the best card those whom republicans
call 'rejectionist' unionists have in their hand.

It totally justifies their refusal to share power;
it embarrasses moderate unionism and
pushes wavering unionists into the hands of those who would just
return Northern Ireland to the past.

And because it also embarrasses the British and Irish
governments,
it makes it harder for us to respond to nationalist concerns.

To this blunt question:
'How come the Irish government won't allow Sinn Fein to be in
government in the South until the IRA ceases its activity,
but unionists must have them in government in the North?'
There are many sophisticated answers.

But no answer is as simple, telling and direct as the question.
So: that's where we are.
Not another impasse.
But a fundamental choice of direction, a turning point.

*Tony Blair, Northern Ireland, 18 October 2002*

### 4 One sentence per paragraph

Yes, the current stalemate is a crisis, a dangerous crisis.

But it is not a crisis that began one week ago outside a bar in Belfast.

It is not a crisis around the IRA or IRA intentions.

The institutions have been suspended now for almost eighteen months.

This is the fourth suspension.

In the same period the IRA have taken a number of initiatives to move the process forward, whereas both governments, and particularly the British government, have failed repeatedly to deliver on their commitments.

In the same period the securocrats have succeeded in stalling the process of change.

But that is all they have managed to do.

They have not halted this process, nor have they reversed it.

Nor will we allow them to.

We have negotiated, and campaigned and argued to have the Good Friday Agreement implemented not only because that is our obligation, not only because it is the right thing, but also because it fits into a strategy of providing and maintaining a political alternative to conflict, a means of sustaining and anchoring the peace process and a transition to the free independent Ireland we have worked long to achieve.

That is what our negotiations strategy is about.

That is what we will continue to do.

Sinn Fein is in this process to the end.

Our intention is clear.

Our intention is peaceful.

Our intention is to succeed.

*Martin McGuinness, Sinn Fein Annual Conference, March 2004.*

You may need three versions of the speech: one for the speaker, one for distribution and one for transfer to autocue. Fix the pages firmly for the speaker. Many a speaker has lost a page over the front of the lectern – or turned one and come to a blank. It happened to Nigel Lawson during his 1987 Budget speech. He recollected:

> *When I reached the passage in question, I saw immediately that the text skipped a page, so I improvised from memory while looking for the missing page . . . Fortunately my memory of the missing page was pretty good, so my improvisation was very close to the actual text which I found pretty soon – although it seemed longer – and no harm was done . . . Although it was a nasty moment, I was able to keep cool and unflustered partly because I was accustomed to this sort of pressure.*[10]

Perhaps you know the story about the speaker with the disgruntled speechwriter? He was orating his lengthy speech when he came to a page that was blank but for the words, 'You're on your own now, you bastard.'

A file or folder is useful at the dispatch box or a lectern. The Queen has fancy folders for speeches; otherwise she uses a Treasury tag, which is perfect: the turned pages lie flat. Making a speech is an ordeal for almost anyone, so the final stages of preparation may become a ritual. The right paper, layout, fastening, folder and pen all help the speaker feel more comfortable and confident.

### Distribution copies

It helps to add a title by which the speech can be remembered. It may be purely functional – 'The Chancellor's 2004 Budget Speech' – or more evocative, such as 'Their Finest Hour', or 'The Wind of

Change', but not so mysterious that nobody will ever quite know what it means, such as the 'The British Dream' or 'Shifting the Balance of Power in the NHS'.

## Autocue

An autocue allows a speaker to follow a script without having to read from a sheaf of paper. A couple of clear glass plates the size of a tea tray are set at an angle on either side of the lectern. To the audience, they are transparent, but to the speaker they are more like mirrors, with the words projected up from floor level and appearing line by line on both glass plates at the same time. The speaker's head moves from side to side, not up and down, so they appear to be maintaining eye-contact with the audience. Behind the scenes, a computer operator projects the full text of the speech, line by line, controlling the speed of the words' appearance. A speech from an autocue has to be read verbatim.

There's a scene in the film *Speechless* that demonstrates how an autocue works. Michael Keaton and Geena Davis play speechwriters for rival political parties. One sabotages the other's autocue, so that the speaker ends up talking rubbish. This actually happened to Harriet Harman, at the Labour Party conference in 1997: 'All these unfamiliar words started coming up on the autocue. I couldn't go back to my notes, and just had to carry on. I realised that Gordon Brown had made the changes and deleted all my references to spending plans.'[11]

## Taking to the podium . . .

So now, speechwriter, all you can do is watch. Speaker, you must walk slowly to the podium, taking time to assess the audience. Sometimes, the audience will be waiting. At others, they will be chatting so the speaker has to quieten them. This can be scary. One option is to raise the voice, say, 'Ladies and gentlemen [or whatever],' and wait for silence. Another option – and it doesn't work for everyone but is well worth trying – is to stand as still as a statue, establishing eye-contact with individuals. It gives you time to adjust to the venue, and more time to assess the situation. Eventually the audience will be silent.

## The first few words

Of all the techniques we have looked at in this book, learning the first few lines by heart is one of the simplest, yet most effective ways to get a speech off to a good start. It boosts the speaker's confidence and quickly establishes their rapport with the audience.

I remember accompanying a speaker to a major conference at the Institute of Directors at the Albert Hall. The setting was dramatic – white lights on black staging, whose edges merged into the darkness of the auditorium. The speaker came to the podium, said a few words, hesitated, said a few more, stumbled and eventually got going about halfway down the first page of the script. The problem, he told me later, was that as he walked on to the stage he had been dazzled by the lights and had to wait until his eyes adjusted.

If the speaker has learnt the first lines there is less chance that he or she will say something unscripted that they may later regret. This was what happened to Tony Blair at the start of his speech to the Women's Institute in 2000.[12] The first words of his script were: 'The Women's Institute is a powerful force for good.' At worst this would have been soporific. What he said was: 'This is truthfully the most terrifying audience I've ever seen in my life,' provoking a mixture of embarrassed laughter and disapproving silence. That was where the trouble started. Then he failed to engage the audience, either personally or collectively:

*My argument to you today is that the renewal of community is the answer to the challenges of a changing world. The way we do it is to combine the old and the new, traditional British values of responsibility and respect for others, with a new agenda of opportunity for all in a changing world.*

The pleasantries he made about the Women's Institute failed to reveal anything about the audience that they didn't already know. They soon lost patience. On page six of his eleven-page script he started on the health service. The slow handclapping started. Unable to talk through it, he looked up from his script, and said: 'I have spent a long time trying to work very hard on the National Health Service.'

The audience was unpitying. He bit his lip, looked nervous, glanced at the chair for reassurance. She intervened, but the damage was done. Soon after, he concluded his speech and left the stage.

The Women's Institute complained that Blair had broken their rules by giving a political speech. But when we look more closely we can see that the audience reacted from the outset to a series of serious flaws on the drafting and delivery. He caused the reaction he got.

It was rather different from what Bill Clinton continued with after his introduction to the 2002 Labour Party Conference:

*I am sort of getting used to being the spouse of an elected official instead of one, but it is flattering when someone who no longer has a shred of power is asked what he thinks, so I thought I would show up and say. It is also fun to be in a place where our crowd is still in office and I am glad to be here. But the real reason I came here today is because politics matters. It matters to the people whom you represent, and because we live in an interdependent world what you do here matters to all of us across the globe. I have just come here from a trip to Africa,*

*which provided me with all kinds of fresh evidence of the
importance of politics.*

In fairness to Blair, his wasn't a political speech in the sense of it being
a Labour Party speech: it was a governmental speech about vision,
policy and achievement, which are surely legitimate topics for prime
ministers to address. Most of it was about a vision of values in British
society: 'Opportunity to all and responsibility from all equals a
community for all.' Blair had prepared the speech himself while on
paternity leave following the birth of his son, Leo. The journalist Polly
Toynbee called it an 'interminable tract, replete with slogans, sancti-
mony, aphorisms, and lists of self-praising statistics', and declared that
it should be 'the last of its outdated kind'.[14] The Prime Minister was
safe to assume that the content of the speech would be soon forgotten,
for he used the same themes but in a world context in his Labour
Party Conference speech the following year: 'The moral power of the
world acting as a community'; 'Not each person for themselves, but
working together as a community to ensure that everyone, not just the
privileged few get the chance to succeed'. And Polly Toynbee declared:
'Language is a powerful weapon of war and the Prime Minister
wielded it faultlessly. It was the speech of a lifetime.'[15]

## Interventions, questions and hecklers

To avoid the fiasco at the Women's Institute, Tony Blair should have
prepared and learnt by heart a charming, uniting first few words. He
should have prepared the sort of speech the audience wanted to hear.
The unscripted appeal that he had been 'thinking about the NHS'
would have been better unsaid. When the slow handclap started, he
could perhaps have switched to a different theme. But, realistically,
his only option was to end.

Everybody deals with interventions in their own way. Some speakers relish them: they know that snatching triumph from near disaster makes them heroic. Most would prefer to avoid interventions, so always make a risk assessment (see pages 127-128) during your preparation for a speech. Think of what may go wrong and how to use it creatively.

An audience tends to be on the side of a speaker who makes a good-natured effort to deal with whatever problems come up. It can quickly turn against a speaker who gets rattled. The aim in dealing with interventions, questions and heckling is to keep the audience on your side.

Questions – whether within the speech or at the end – are a great opportunity to talk with the audience, rather than at them. Deal with them at face value and reply to the whole audience. If the topic has already been dealt with but the questioner seems to have missed it, calmly repeat what you've already said as if for the first time. Check that the questioner is satisfied with your reply before you move on. If you don't know the answer, say so, then tell them you'd need more information than you have with you to give a complete answer, that you will come back to them – and do so.

Canny speakers work out in advance a strategy for dealing with interruptions. Legitimate interventions can work in a speaker's favour, if only by reducing the opposition's speaking time in a debate. Ignore interruptions only if you can trust the organisers to deal with them. Otherwise, improvise. If the interruption is a technical hitch, anything from a powercut to a bomb scare, think first of the safety of the audience and the extent to which you must control the subsequent events. The most common hitch – the microphone failing – can be a blessing. Speak up, check that the people at the back can hear, talk trustingly about the technicians who are fixing the problem and carry on. The audience will appreciate your efforts. When a heckler interrupts, respond to the whole audience. It is better to say something safe, dull and forgettable than to come out with an unforgettable barb you may later regret. Witty put-downs have a legitimate use but only when the audience has turned against the heckler.

If you run out of time, don't admit it, simply précis the final few topics. If possible, hint that you'd be prepared to take questions on those later topics. If you detect that the audience is lost, cut the speech short by outlining the remainder and finish early.

The more speeches you make or listen to, the larger your repertory of disaster stories: powercuts, drills, collapsing scenery, fire alarms, bomb scares, protesters, eggs, rats and rain. Learning how to deal with them is a mixture of preparation and practice. Take them in your stride and you take the audience with you.

### The expert listener

You are an expert listener who could recognise a good speech long before you read this book. And listeners can rid the world of dreary speeches. Nobody should have to sit through them. Listeners can advise the organisers – the speakers too if they get the chance – that they would like to be involved rather than talked at.

Those who feel that anyone who uses the tools in this book is to be distrusted should perhaps spare a generous thought for the speaker. Maybe he or she used them for your benefit, to make what they say enjoyable and interesting.

Next time you feel moved by a speech, or convinced, or won over, or swept along, ask yourself why. You now know much more about why the speech had that effect and will be able to identify the specific causes. As Bill Clinton observed, 'All politics is a combination of rhetoric and reality . . . at some point you've to look at the evidence.'[16] Above all, remember that the ability to listen is as important as the ability to speak.

# Frequently asked questions about speeches

1.          What is a good speech?

Words that connect a speaker, an audience, a subject, an occasion, a time and a place.

2.          What makes a good speaker?

Empathy, vision, passion, realism, and the skill to communicate all of those.

3.          Why should I give a speech?

For leadership. To make an occasion special. It's (nearly always) better than a presentation. (See also chapter 1, pages 4–7.)

4.          What should my speech be about?

The real question is: what is your speech for?

5.          How do I start?

With how you feel. With something you and the audience are interested in and agree on. With an unusual image or fact. (See also chapter 2, pages 18–27.)

6.    What shall I say in the middle?

Answer three questions of interest to you and the audience. (See chapters 4 and 6, pages 71–72, and 120–127.)

7.    How do I get them cheering in the aisles?

Speak with passion, sincerity, empathy and reality. Use the tools described in chapter 3 (pages 42–45).

8.    How do I end?

With a glimpse of the future. With a thought to take away. With a round of applause (see pages 37–38).

9.    How do I write a speech for someone else?

Get to know your speaker and understand some short-cuts by referring to chapters 5 and 7 (pages 103–119 and 140).

10.    How long should a speech be?

Long enough to do the job. Short enough to keep your audience's interest. (See chapter 2, pages 17–19.)

11.    How many words a minute?

120 is the average. (See chapter 8, page 155.)

12.    Help! I've only five minutes to work on my speech draft!

'Get your ducks lined up' – make sure your content does the job. Give it an image. Include a quotable quote. Learn the first sentence by heart. If you find more time, see chapter 8 (page 157.)

13.    How do I overcome stage fright?

Practice giving more smaller speeches. On the day, think of the audience as being one friendly person. Be yourself. (See chapter 8, pages 152-154.)

# Notes

Chapter 1: Speeches still matter...

1 Members of the Welsh Assembly have computers they can use to email each other during debates, but essentially business is done with speeches.

2 Benn, Tony, Channel 4 Political Awards, 1999.

3 Lord Hutton, statement on the publication of his report of the inquiry into the death of weapons expert Dr David Kelly, 28 January 2004.

4 Stemp, Leslie, *Speeches and Toasts*, Ward, Lock, 1950, p.15.

Chapter 2: What makes a good speech and how to build one

1 The first lines from Leo Tolstoy's *Anna Karenina*.

2 Annan, Kofi, Nobel lecture, 10 December 2001.

3 Prescott, John, Launch of the 'Your Say' campaign in Warrington, 4 November 2003.

4 Major, John, *The Autobiography*, Harper Collins, 1999, p.32-3.

5 Spencer, Charles, oration at the funeral of Diana, Princess of Wales, 6 September 1997.

6 Clinton, Bill, Labour Party Conference, 2 October 2002.

7 Cook, Robin, resignation speech, House of Commons, *Hansard*, 17 March 2003, col.726.

8 Kelly, Patrick, Roman Catholic Archbishop of Liverpool, remembrance service for the victims of the Morecambe Bay tragedy, 23 February 2004.

9 Bush, George, radio address, 15 September 2001.

10 An adaptation of the 'Situation, Complication, Question, Answer' formula, devised by

Barbara Minto in *The Pyramid Principle, Logic in Writing and Thinking*, Pitman, 1987.

11 Bush, George, television address, 7 October 2001.

12 Cooke, Alistair, *Letter from America*, BBC Radio 4, 9 March 2003.

13 Anon, *After Dinner Speeches, Toasts and Stories,* Foulsham, 1998.

14 Blair, Cherie, statement, 11 December 2002.

15 *Daily Telegraph*, 12 December 2002.

16 Blair, Tony, statement following the death of Diana, Princess of Wales, 31 August 1997.

17 King, Martin Luther, Washington, DC, 28 August 1963.

18 Weather Forecast, BBC Radio 4, 19 October 2003

19 Thatcher, Margaret, Conservative Party Conference, 10 October 1975.

20 Carnegie, Dale, *The Quick and Easy Way to Effective Speaking*, Mandarin, 1990, a revised edition by Dorothy Carnegie of *Public Speaking and Influencing Men in Business*, 1920, p.122-3.

21 Kennedy, Charles, House of Commons, *Hansard*, col.349.

22 Bush, George, addressing a joint session of Congress, 20 September 2001.

23 Bin Laden, Osama, as translated in the *Guardian*, 8 October 2001.

24 Blair, Tony, Labour Party Conference, 28 September 1999.

Chapter 3: Words

1 Queen Elizabeth I, Tilbury, 9 August 1588.

2 Armstrong, Neil, on landing on the moon, 21 July 1969.

3 Kennedy, John F., Inaugural address, 20 January 1961.

4 '*Veni, vidi, vici*', Julius Caesar, *Divus Julius*, 37.2, CE 55

5 Churchill, Winston, House of Commons, 4 June 1940.

6 King, Martin Luther, Washington, DC, 28 August 1963.

7 Churchill, Winston, House of Commons and radio address, 18 June 1940.

8 Blair, Tony, Labour Party Conference, 28 September 1999.

9 Bush, George, State of the Union Address, 29 January 2002.

10 Mandela, Nelson, during his trial, Johannesburg, 20 April 1964.

11 Gandhi, Mahatma, during his trial, Ahmadabad, 23 March 1922.

12  Lincoln, Abraham, Gettysburg Address, 19 November 1863.

13  Blair, Tony, Labour Party Conference, 1 October 1996.

14  Major, John, media statement, 22 June 1995.

15  First used during the *World This Weekend*, BBC Radio 4, 10 Jan 1993.

16  Major, John, statement on entering 10 Downing Street, 28 November 1990.

17  Portillo, Michael, Conservative Party Conference, 3 October 2000.

18  King, Martin Luther, Washington, DC, 28 August 1963.

19  Kinnock, Neil, Bridgend, 7 June 1983.

20  Thatcher, Margaret, Conservative Party Conference, 10 October 1975.

21  Pankhurst, Emmeline, London, 24 March 1908.

22  Blair, Tony, Royal Festival Hall, 2 May 1997.

23  Benn, Tony, House of Commons, *Hansard*, 17 February 1998, col. 926. See also
    chapter 4 page 94.

24  Mandela, Nelson, 10 May 1994.

25  The Prince of Wales, *Thought for the Day*, BBC Radio 4, 1 January 2000.

26  Atkinson, Max, *Our Masters' Voices: The Language and Body Language of Politics*,
    Methuen, 1984, pp.203

27  Bush, George, State of the Union address, 20 January 2004.

28  Bush, George, radio address, 15 September 2001.

29  Brown, Gordon, Labour Party Conference, 30 September 2000.

30  Benn, Tony, accepting from the Speaker of the House, Betty Boothroyd, Channel 4's
    award for Parliamentary Speechmaker of the Year, 20 March 1999.

31  Blair, Tony, Earth Summit, Johannesburg, 1-2 September 2002.

32  *Daily Telegraph*, 5 May 2004.

33  Clinton, Bill, Labour Party Conference, 2 October 2002.

34  Duncan Smith, Iain, Conservative Party Conference, 11 October 2002.

35  Major, John, speech to Conservative Group for Europe, 22 April 1993.

36  The Queen, Ghana, 8 November 1999.

37  Stemp, Leslie, *Speeches and Toasts*, Ward Lock, 1950, p.55.

38  The Queen, Lord Mayor of London's Banquet, 24 November 1992.

39  Gerard Russell, quoted by Anton La Guardia in *Daily Telegraph*, 1 April 2003.

40  Hague, William, Conservative Party Conference, 9 October 2001.

41  The Queen, Golden Jubilee Lunch, Guildhall, 4 June 2002.

42  McGimpsey, Michael, *Belfast Telegraph*, 16 February 2000.

43  Atkinson, Max, ibid, p.31.

44  *Star Trek*, NBC from 1966 onwards, now Paramount.

45  Bower, Rachel, pers. comm.

46  Thatcher, Margaret, Conservative Party Conference, 11 October 1980.

47  Llewelyn-Bowen, Laurence, National Trust Lecture, 4 March 2003.

48  Milburn, Alan, 'Shifting the Balance of Power in NHS', 25 April 2001.

49  Benn, Tony, *The Times*, 24 March 2004.

Chapter 4: Special occasions

1  *Calendar Girls*, Touchstone Pictures, 2003.

2  Waite, Terry, in *On This Day*, BBC News Archive, www.news.bbc.co.uk.

3  Waite, Terry, *Taken on Trust*, Hodder and Stoughton, 1993, p.359-61.

4  Carnegie, Dale, *The Quick and Easy Way to Effective Speaking*, Mandarin, 1990, a revised edition by Dorothy Carnegie of *Public Speaking and Influencing Men in Business*, 1920, p.213-4.

5  Parris, Matthew, Channel 4 Political awards, Channel 4 Television, 20 March 2002.

6  Portillo, Michael, 2 May 1997.

7  Tolkein, J.R.R., *Lord of the Rings, part 1, The Fellowship of the Ring*, 1954, Unwin edition, 1966, p.36-7. The 2001 film by New Line Cinema/Wingnut Productions includes an edited version.

8  *Four Weddings and a Funeral*, Columbia Tristar, 1994.

9  Fairclough, Norman, *New Labour, New Language?*, Routledge, 2000, p.51-65.

10  Benn, Tony, House of Commons, *Hansard*, 17 February 1998, col. 926.

11  Blair, Tony, House of Commons, *Hansard*, 24 September 2002, col. 1.

12  Cook, Robin, House of Commons, *Hansard*, 17 March 2003, col. 726.

13  Debate on the Queen's speech, House of Commons, *Hansard*, 30 October 1996, cols 660 and 674.

Chapter 5: Hearts and minds

1   Blair, Tony, 'The British Labour Party Today', Perth University, Australia, 1982, repro-
    duced in *Tony Blair In His Own Words*, Paul Richards (ed.), Politico's, 2004.

2   *Braveheart*, 20th Century Fox, 1995.

3   Clinton, Bill, television address after testifying to Grand Jury, 17 August 1998.

4   Honey, Peter and Mumford, A., *The manual of learning styles*, Peter Honey, 1986.

5   Goffee, Robert, and Jones, Gareth, 'Why Should Anyone Be Led By You?', in *Harvard
    Business Review*, vol. 78, 2000, p.62-70.

6   Goffee, Robert, and Jones, Gareth, 'Followership', in *Harvard Business Review*, vol 79,
    2001, p.148.

7   Collins, Lt Col Tim, addressing the 1st Battalion Royal Irish Regiment, Iraq, 19 March
    2003.

8   Tannen, Deborah, *You Just Don't Understand: Women and Men in Conversation*, Virago,
    1991.

9   Howard, Michael, *Policy Exchange*, 9 February 2004.

10  Goffee, Robert, and Jones, Gareth, 'Why Should Anyone Be Led By You?', *Harvard
    Business Review*, vol. 78, 2000, p.68.

11  Monkhouse, Bob, *Just Say a Few Words*, Lennard, 1999, p.36.


Chapter 6: Research

1   Blair, Tony, general election announcement, 8 May 2001.

2   Greenfield, Baroness Susan, 'The Brain of the Future', Royal Institution, 16 May 2002.

3   Greenfield, Baroness Susan, House of Lords, *Hansard*, 21 November 2001, Col.1192.

4   *The Times*, 9 March 2000.


Chapter 7: The speechwriter and the client

1   De Vita, Emma, in *Management Today*, May 2003, p.64.

2    Peggy Noonan, interviewed for *Strictly Speaking*, BBC Radio 4, 28 May 2003.

3    Michael Portillo, interviewed for *Strictly Speaking*, BBC Radio 4, 28 May 2003.

4    Matthew Parris, interviewed for *Strictly Speaking*, BBC Radio 4, 28 May 2003.

5    Major, John, *The Autobiography*, Harper Collins, 1999, p.32-3.

6    Frum, David, *Westminster Hour*, BBC Radio 4, 26 April 2003.

7    Churchill, Winston, 18 June 1940.

8    Currie, Edwina, *A Parliamentary Affair*, Hodder and Stoughton, 1993, p.168-9.

Chapter 8: Giving and receiving a speech

1    Research into the links between voice, gesture, and message are discussed by Geoffrey Beattie in *Visible Thought*, Routledge, 2003.

2    Winston, Robert, *The Human Mind*, Bantam Press, 2003, p.300-306.

3    Brogan, Benedict, *Daily Telegraph*, 14 August 2003.

4    Powell, Colin, presentation to the UN Security Council, 5 February 2003.

5    Anon, *After Dinner Speeches, Toasts and Stories*, Foulsham, 1998, p.31.

6    *New York Times*, 28 January 2003.

7    Major, John, interview with Anthony Seldon, from *John Major; A Political Life*, Phoenix, 1997.

8    Widdecombe, Ann, Conservative Party Conference, 6 October 1998.

9    Rozenberg, Gabriel, *The Times*, London, 3 May 2004.

10  Lawson, Nigel, *The View from No. 11*, Bantam Press, 1992, p.688.

11  Rentoul, John, *Tony Blair*, Warner, 2001, p.373. The original source quoted as *Sunday Mirror*, 3 October 1999.

12  Blair, Tony, 7 June 2000.

13  Clinton, Bill, Labour Party Conference, 2 October 2002.

14  Toynbee, Polly, the *Guardian*, 9 June 2000.

15  Toynbee, Polly, the *Guardian*, 3 October 2001.

16  Clinton, Bill, Labour Party Conference, 2 October 2002.

# Index